Crafts of Israel

Crafts of Israel

Ruth Dayan

with

Wilburt Feinberg

MACMILLAN PUBLISHING CO., INC.
NEW YORK

COLLIER MACMILLAN PUBLISHERS
LONDON

Macmillan Publishing Co., Inc.
866 Third Avenue, New York, N.Y. 10022
Collier-Macmillan Canada Ltd.

Book design: Herbert M Rosenthal

Library of Congress Catalog Card Number:
73–10787

First Printing 1974

Printed in the United States of America

**To all those who made
a place in the world
for Israeli crafts**

There were many who gave of their time and thoughts so that this book would ''come to form.'' We wish especially to acknowledge the help of Loretta Eskenazi, a new immigrant from Greece; Yaki Molho, a sabra born in Tel Aviv whose parents came from Greece; and Helga Dudman, journalist of *The Jerusalem Post,* for their assistance throughout the writing of this book. Their contributions have made possible this presentation of Israeli crafts, and we deeply thank them.

CONTENTS

1 Sabra plant
Courtesy: The Israel Government Tourist Office

During the early 1950s Israel experienced large-scale immigration from both east and west, and the practical problems of building our country were vast. It was not easy at that time to ensure the development of Israeli crafts a place among the country's priorities. Few envisaged then that through the stormy history of these past two decades there would emerge the wealth of talent that has so determinedly burst forth.

Under the guidance of Ruth Dayan, whose unselfish and uncompromising efforts set the pace, we tried to find the best way to preserve and expand our limited resources of traditional crafts through the further development of arts and crafts. This way has been found, and the work of our craftsmen reaches the far corners of the world.

I feel it of great significance that the story of these efforts—the story of our people and their work—will now be brought forth. We are confident that the strong will and determination of the past will bring even greater success in the future.

Teddy Kollek
Mayor of Jerusalem

2 Aerial view of Jerusalem's Western Wall
showing the proximity of the wall to
the Dome of the Rock
Courtesy: The Zionist Archives and Library

This is an ideal time in the history of Israel for a book about its crafts. It is a time of interweaving of patterns of varied cultures—a time of a great influx of people and a meeting of many different worlds. This exodus has been described and analyzed many times, and the history of the rebirth of Israel is best left to others. The purpose of this book is to portray the Israeli craftsman of yesterday and today and his work.

Whether a sabra (native-born Israeli) or from Yemen, North or South Africa, Holland, Germany, Russia, or any of the many countries from which our people have come, the Israeli craftsman is influenced by the land. Craftsmen have borrowed colors from the cobalt sky, the fields of citron, olive, and date, the sands of the Negev, the sun-baked hills, and the gold of Jerusalem; they have taken the shapes of the Bedouin tent, the roaring sea, and the shallow hills. They have mixed these colors and shapes into a new creation, which is a reflection of Israel itself.

Immigrating craftsmen have brought with them skills and traditions that were acquired in the Balkans, Persia, Bukhara, Romania, and other lands. They have brought their native crafts of carpet weaving, gold and silver working, embroidery, wood carving, dressmaking, ceramics, glass making, and many other techniques and talents developed by generations of experience. Much of this reservoir of skill brought to Israel would surely have disappeared without encouragement and the opportunity to put it to use. Israel offered both, and these skills, fused together into the current Israeli amalgam, were to produce its children and its craftsmen. Readers of this book will spend a few moments in the lives of these people.

There will also be moments from the past because to learn about anything current in Israel is also to refer to the past. Although the authors make no attempt at a comprehensive history, it must be stressed that the historic Israel plays a very important role in present and future Israeli crafts and cannot be overlooked.

What is Israeli craft? A unique assemblage of many different people working with many different materials, working with their hands and hearts to create works of beauty. Through hard work, talent, and much experience, an Israeli style is gradually emerging. It is a style based on imported skills, shaped and colored by Israel's history and the land itself. It is influenced as well by the archaeological discoveries of ancient objects and the world of myth, symbolism, and fantastically rich imagery found in the stories of the Bible and the biblical treasury of knowledge and wisdom. These are the roots of Israel's crafts and from them the genesis of an Israeli style.

Handcrafts, like all other arts, are the representatives of a nation's cultural personality, and Israeli crafts are unique; they are unlike those of any other nation. It has taken many years for the emergence of a style—a presentation that only Israel has to offer—to take its place in the world of crafts. It is not only the skill of fabrication that produces a work of art; it is the originality of view that derives from the creator that is distinctly the crafts of Israel.

Israel is located at one of the crossroads of the world. It has been home to conquerors and vanquished alike, and they have stored their cultures in its arid earth. With the waves of peoples from other lands came craftsmen and styles that have left their mark even on the landscape. Walk along the shoreline, kick at the sand. It will often reveal a bit of pottery, glass, or metal—souvenir of a glorious past. Many of the craftsmen returned to their native lands, but Israel remains—Israel with this buried beauty to discover and explore and to inspire the imagination of its craftsmen.

During one short period of recent development there seemed to be few imaginative ideas and more kitsch. Fortunately this trend has disappeared and a crafts quality that is exciting and pleasurable has emerged.

The collection of crafts shown in this book is representative of the work of Israeli craftsmen; it does not pretend to encompass all Israeli crafts. Unfortunately the work of every craftsman is not within these pages; the omissions are regrettable. But every day new techniques are developed and new craftsmen appear.

4000–3200 B.C.E. **CHALCOLITHIC PERIOD**
Ghassulian culture
Open villages
Copper industry
Underground dwellings
Round, apsidal, and rectangular houses
Highly developed art—ivory, copper, stone, frescoes

3200–2200 B.C.E. **EARLY CANAANITE (BRONZE) PERIOD**
Cultural contacts with Egypt, Mesopotamia, Anatolia, Cyprus
Fortified urban settlements, sanctuaries, and high places

2200–1500 B.C.E. **MIDDLE CANAANITE (BRONZE) PERIOD**
THE AGE OF THE PATRIARCHS
Strong political and cultural ties with Egypt
Hyksos rule in Egypt
Small city-states
Strongly fortified cities
Horses and war chariots in Canaan and Egypt
Beginnings of pictographic writing
Development of ceramic and metal industries
First mention of Jerusalem in Egyptian inscription

1500–1200 B.C.E. **LATE CANAANITE (BRONZE) PERIOD**
Egyptian domination of Canaan and administration based on
Canaanite petty kingdoms
Amarna Age
Exodus and conquest of Canaan by Israelite tribes: Moses and
Joshua
Extensive international trade
Alphabetic writing

1200–1000 B.C.E. **ISRAELITE (IRON) PERIOD I**
Invasion of the Sea People
Settlement in Canaan of Israelite tribes
Period of the Judges
Philistine city-states

1000–587 B.C.E. **ISRAELITE (IRON) PERIOD II**
United monarchy: Saul, David, Solomon
Struggle with Philistines
Political expansion of Israel at its peak
Economic prosperity: mining, foreign trade
Ties with Phoenicia
Divided monarchy: Kingdoms of Judah and Israel
Fall of Samaria (722 B.C.E.)
Kingdom of Judah
Struggle between Egypt and Assyria
Destruction of Jerusalem and First Temple (587 B.C.E.)
Development of fortifications and warfare
Phoenician and Aramaean influences
The Prophets

587–332 B.C.E. **PERSIAN PERIOD**
Neo-Babylonian Period (587–537 B.C.E.)
Persian domination from 537 B.C.E.
Cyrus's edict on Jewish rights
Return from Babylonian captivity
Ezra and Nehemiah
Building of the Second Temple and the Walls of Jerusalem
Judah autonomous within Persian Empire
Rule of the High Priests and the Great Assembly at Jerusalem

332–37 B.C.E. HELLENISTIC PERIOD HASMONAEAN DYNASTY
Rule of Ptolemies and Seleucids
Foundation of Hellenistic cities
Hellenization of country and religious reaction in the Maccabean period
Maccabean War of Liberation
Hasmonaean Dynasty
Pompey's conquest (63 B.C.E.): beginning of Roman rule
Earlier Apocrypha
Septuagint
Dead Sea Scrolls

37 B.C.E.–132 C.E. HERODIAN PERIOD ROMAN PERIOD I
Hellenistic-Roman culture in country
Herodian Dynasty: Roman governors (Pontius Pilate)
Jesus and beginning of Christianity
First war against the Romans
Dead Sea Scrolls
Destruction of Jerusalem and Second Temple (70 C.E.)
Jewish religious center at Yavne

132–135 C.E. BAR KOKHBA
Second war against Rome
Bar Kokhba Letters

73–324 C.E. ROMAN PERIOD II–III
Completion of the Mishnah
General crisis in third century: decline of agriculture; inflation and barbarian invasions; recovery of the empire under Diocletian and Constantine
Roman theaters: Caesarea, Beit Shearim
Early synagogues
Jewish Diaspora

324–640 C.E. BYZANTINE PERIOD
Rule by Byzantine Empire
Completion of Jerusalem Talmud
Synagogues and Churches
Development of mosaic art

640–1099 C.E. EARLY ARAB PERIOD
Rise of Islam
Arab conquest of country
Foundation of Ramleh
Building of Dome of the Rock (Omar Mosque)

1099–1187 C.E. CRUSADER PERIOD
Christian conquest of the country
Establishment of the Latin language
Kingdom of Jerusalem
Rebuilding of the Holy Sepulchre and other churches
Building of many castles: Acre, Atlit, Montfort, and others

3 Candelabra sculpted in stone
Bet Shearim Catacombs
Courtesy: The Zionist Archives and Library

TRUTH SPRINGETH OUT
OF THE EARTH . . . PSALMS 85:12

... אמת מארץ תצמח

1 THE PAST

I t is often easy to understand phenomena clearly in retrospect, after time has passed and the subject can be studied in the context of its history. Fortunately, in Israel the past and the present are one. The sights of past cultures are found everywhere and can be explored without difficulty. Archaeological expeditions are common, and only because of the lack of funds are they not at every corner.

To the historian the extraordinary influence of Israel on the world has always been a paradox. This small and poor land has produced Judaism and Christianity and has had a decisive influence on the development of Islam. Through these religions the land has exercised unparalleled influence on the course of man's activity for more than two thousand years. To be sure, from Greece, also a small and poor land, emerged the intellectual life and an artistic concept of beauty which have conditioned all subsequent Western culture and history. But Greece had become wealthy through its far-spreading commerce before the flowering of the Hellenic spirit (332 B.C.E.–73 C.E.), and it remained wealthy throughout its Golden Age. Israel, on the contrary, was always a poor country; its periods of relative prosperity were few and brief. Though historians and philosophers have been unable to resolve so profound a paradox, we can at least review some of the facts that make it easier to recognize the unusual suitability of the Holy Land for its role.

Because of its historical role, Israel provides us with examples of crafts made during great and ordinary times. We know that the Israeli peasant and craftsman of the age of Elijah (1000 B.C.E.) had far better tools at his disposal than his predecessors. Instead of the wooden sickles with flint-lined edges used in 1500 B.C.E. by the sons of Jacob to reap grain there were sharp iron sickles, and twice as much grain could be reaped in the same time. It is true that

5   Glass vessels of the Roman period
Two unguentaria (free blown), juglet of Sidonian style (mold blown), ribbed bowl (mold pressed)
All: Early Roman Imperial period
The invention, probably at Sidon, of a technique for glass making either in molds or free blown allowed for the first time the mass production of delicate and cheap glass vessels.
Photo: David Harris
Courtesy: The Israel Museum, Jerusalem

6

the reaper had to grasp the ears of grain with one hand as he severed the grain head from the stalks—just as in Egyptian relief paintings. The day of the long scythe was far in the future. The carpenter had iron tools of every kind. He used large iron axes and adzes to cut down trees and trim beams or boards; he had thin iron saws in frames similar to modern bucksaws that were much cheaper and more durable than copper saws and files. Great sledge hammers and little chisels and gouges were also made from iron. The wealth that poured into the Canaanite (Phoenician) cities on the coast of northern Israel from all parts of the ancient world made possible the development of a form of production technology that can be compared with modern conveyor-belt manufacture as versus older machine production. A comparison of Israeli pottery of Iron Age II (1000 B.C.E.) with Middle Bronze (2000 B.C.E.) ware is very instructive in this respect. In spite of the care and artistic skill devoted to making individual pieces in the Middle Bronze Age, the rapid fabrication ware of the ninth–seventh centuries B.C.E. produced items much better suited to their functional purposes.

It is interesting to study the articles used by women in a typical Israelite site and to contrast them with objects from a site that dates only slightly earlier. In the older site you can usually find rough, locally made jewelry; in the Israelite site corresponding articles are made of cheap materials but by cleverly skilled craftsmen. The Israelites had little round palettes of hard limestone for use in preparing face paint and cosmetics; the margins are covered with accurate geometric designs far superior in skill of execution to those of the awkward hand-carved designs on wares of earlier times. There are many bone pendants, but they were gracefully turned and were obviously available in large quantities at low prices.

In Israel it is no challenge for the craftsman to know and use the past; the challenge is in how he interprets and translates the past, the present, and the future.

6   Glass container for spice and perfume, 200 C.E.
Photo: Ephraim Kidron

7   Arab gold jewel hoard
Found in glazed pot, the hoard includes: six large gold beads, with granulation; six filigree gold beads, globular and biconical; *(left)* beads, carnelian and glass; *(right)* bronze amulet, with a Koranic verse
The superb craftsmanship of the articles found in the hoard gives a good indication of the highly civilized Islamic city culture in medieval times.
Courtesy: Department of Antiquities, The Israel Museum, Jerusalem

8   Gold jewelry, late Canaanite (bronze) period (1500–1200 B.C.E.)
A and *B:* two toggle pins; *C:* two amulets in the form of flies and pendant possibly representing a larva; *D:* star pendant; *E:* flying hawk amulet; *F:* crescent-shaped amulet; *G:* signet ring bearing the name of Tutakhamon
Courtesy: Department of Antiquities, The Israel Museum, Jerusalem

9   Mesolithic period (c. 10,000–7500 B.C.E.) "natufian"
Bone necklace found in the Carmel region
Courtesy: The Israel Museum, Jerusalem

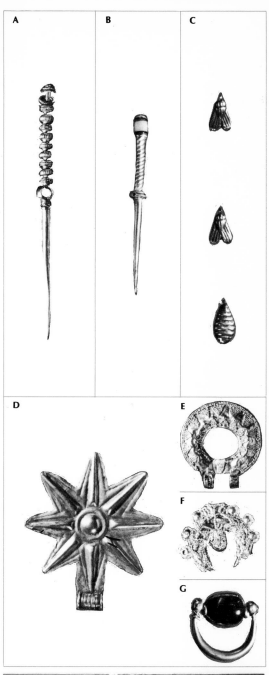

8

9

10

10   Phoenician minor arts
Glass amphoriskos; glass eyebeads;
cosmetic palette and bone spatula, seals,
amulets, weaving implements
All: Israelite period, eighth–sixth
centuries B.C.E. These articles reflect a
high degree of material wealth.
Photo: David Harris
Courtesy: The Israel Museum, Jerusalem

**11   Glass vessels of the Byzantine
period**
In contrast to the functional style of
Roman glass vessels, Byzantine glass is
''baroque'' in form and decoration. The
craftsmen no longer imitated the forms
of ceramic wares but explored the
possibilities of the new medium.
Photo: David Harris
Courtesy: The Israel Museum, Jerusalem

12 Diadem
Gold band set with glass, stone, and
mother-of-pearl third century C.E.
The Barbarian "polychrome" style in
vogue during the latter part of the
Roman Empire and especially in the
Byzantine period was influenced by the
Scythian and Samatian styles of jewelry.
Courtesy: Department of Antiquities, The
Israel Museum, Jerusalem

13 Part of Floor rug (wool), **found at
Masada, Bar Kokhba period (132–135
C.E.)**
Originally the primary colors yellow,
red, and blue were used and mixed to
form different tones and patterns.
Photo: David Harris
Courtesy: Professor Yigael Yadin

13

BY THE RIVERS OF BABYLON, THERE WE SAT

על־נהרות בבל שם ישבנו גם־בכינו בזכרנו את־ציון:

DOWN, YEA, WE WEPT, WHEN WE REMEMBERED

על־ערבים בתוכה תלינו כנורותינו:

ZION. UPON THE WILLOWS IN THE MIDST

כי שם שאלונו שובינו דברי־שיר ותוללינו

THEREOF WE HANGED UP OUR HARPS. FOR

שמחה שירו לנו משיר ציון:

THERE THEY THAT HAD LED US CAPTIVE ASKED

איך נשיר את־שיר־ה׳ על אדמת נכר:

OF US SONG; AND OUR TORMENTORS ASKED

אם־אשכחך ירושלם תשכח ימיני:

OF US MIRTH: 'SING US ONE OF THE SONGS OF

תדבק לשוני לחכי אם־לא אזכרכי אם־לא

ZION.' HOW SHALL WE SING THE LORD'S SONG

אעלה את־ירושלם על ראש שמחתי:

IN A FOREIGN LAND? IF I FORGET THEE, O

JERUSALEM, LET MY RIGHT HAND FORGET HER

CUNNING. IF I REMEMBER THEE NOT,

LET MY TONGUE CLEAVE TO THE ROOF

OF MY MOUTH; IF I SET NOT JERUSALEM

ABOVE MY CHIEFEST JOY. PSALMS 137:1-6

Throughout the many years of the Diaspora the Jewish people never forgot their homeland; they never gave up the idea of the return to Israel. To best understand the dispersion, look at a map of the world; there is no country that has not sheltered a Jewish family. Over the years the movements of the ''wandering Jew'' increased as political and social attitudes changed. The deeply implanted concept of a ''return to Zion,'' the motto of Jews in Diaspora, always remained within the hearts of the Jewish people and was made more intense by the historic drama thrust upon them. The heavy burden of rootlessness led to the mass immigration Israel has received during its recent growth.

In a period of twenty-five years Israel has welcomed over one and a quarter million Jews to its shores—Jews from Yemen and Iraq, immigrants from North Africa and Eastern and Central Europe, and smaller numbers from India, Western Europe, and the Americas. These immigrants came by sea and air

2 TRAVELING

15   Bread baked for Purim Festival
Purim is observed in February or March
in commemoration of the deliverance of
the Jews from the massacre planned by
Haman.
From Morocco

Photo: Sadeh
Courtesy: The Israel Museum, Jerusalem

15

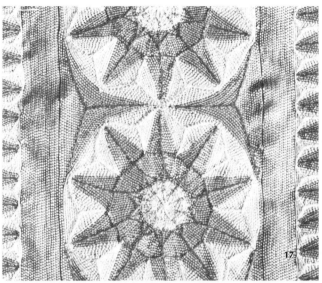

19

20

16 "Gargoush Mezzahar" ceremonial headgear of the Jewish Women of San'a, Yemen
Brocade, cord embroidery, filigree plaques, coins and chains, silver and gilt
Photo: David Harris
Courtesy: The Israel Museum, Jerusalem

17 (Detail) "Kebir" embroidered legging Jewish Women of San'a, Yemen
Detail of embroidery decorating ceremonial trousers; silver thread with red silk
Photo: David Harris
Courtesy: The Israel Museum, Jerusalem

18 (Detail) Yemen woman's cuff from legging brought to Israel
Embroidered with thread and silver beads; peasant style
Courtesy: The Israel Museum, Jerusalem

19 Woman's leather house boots
Made of soft leather
Right: Black calf (plain)
Middle: Appliqué of leather and thread
Left: Embroidery of silver thread on velvet
From Bukhara
Courtesy: The Israel Museum, Jerusalem

20 Woman's leather house boots
Made of soft leather; different colors, appliqué
Photo: David Harris
Courtesy: The Israel Museum, Jerusalem

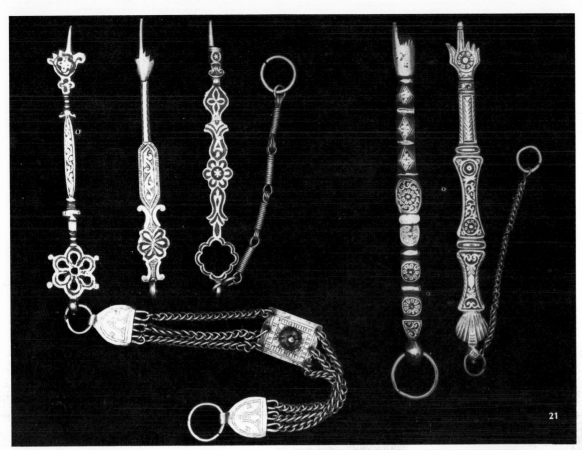

21

22

23

and even by walking across a border. The newcomers joined the Jews who have lived in Israel since the days of the Bible and who have maintained an unbroken connection to a most cherished past. These "old" and "new" Israelis, interweaving their ideas and exchanging techniques and views, laid the foundation for the craft movement in Israel today.

As a segregated minority in other countries, Jews were often forbidden to practice in certain occupations; they were restricted to limited areas of work. However, once these workers arrived in Israel they were able to explore their talents to the fullest. With freedom of expression in every field, these same people achieved proficiency in many areas and grew as part of a development of craftsmanship that has proven successful.

The following maps show where most of our people came from and picture the traditional crafts they brought with them. Many routes were taken, and the journey of their return to Israel was not always by the most direct one. The maps and paths shown are for general information so that those who have not studied the return to Zion can better understand the length, the scope, and the hardships in the journeys of our people.

21 Silver pointers for reading religious books
From Morocco
Photo: Sadeh
Courtesy: The Israel Museum, Jerusalem

22 Jewish seals and designs used in metal decoration
Brought to Israel from Egypt and Morocco (c. 1900)
Photo: Sadeh
Courtesy: The Israel Museum, Jerusalem

23 (Detail) Woman's headwear
Silver and silk thread
From Morocco
Photo: Sadeh
Courtesy: The Israel Museum, Jerusalem

24 Men's Hats
Velvet base with gold thread embroidery
From Bukhara
Courtesy: The Israel Museum, Jerusalem

25 Man's Hat
Embroidered with silk and silver threads
Common to Afghanistan and Bukhara
Photo: David Harris
Courtesy: The Israel Museum, Jerusalem

26 Woman's Hat
Embroidered with gold threads on atlas fabric
From Bukhara
Courtesy: The Israel Museum, Jerusalem

24

25

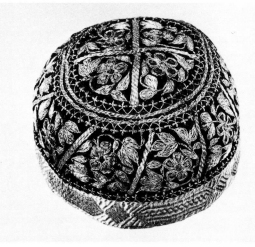
26

AND THE LORD SPOKE UNTO MOSES, SAYING:

וידבר ה׳ אל־משה לאמר:

"SEE, I HAVE CALLED BY NAME BEZALEL,

ראה קראתי בשם בצלאל בן־אורי

THE SON OF URI, THE SON OF HUR, OF THE

בן־חור למטה יהודה:

TRIBE OF JUDAH: AND I HAVE FILLED HIM

ואמלא אתו רוח אלקים בחכמה

WITH THE SPIRIT OF GOD, IN WISDOM, AND IN

ובתבונה ובדעת ובכל־מלאכה:

UNDERSTANDING, AND IN KNOWLEDGE,

לחשב מחשבת לעשות בזהב ובכסף ובנחשת:

AND ALL MANNER OF WORKMANSHIP, TO

ובחרשת אבן למלאת ובחרשת עץ לעשות בכל־מלאכה:

DEVISE SKILFUL WORKS, TO WORK IN GOLD,

AND IN SILVER, AND IN BRASS, AND IN

CUTTING OF STONES FOR SETTING,

AND IN CARVING OF WOOD TO WORK

IN ALL MANNER OF WORKMANSHIP." EXODUS 31:1-5

27 **Bezalel sculpture class (c. 1910)**

3 LEARNING

othing is more carefully enunciated in the Book of Laws, the Torah, than the duty of parents to teach their children the precepts and principles of Judaism. It is also required that the children be taught some practical skill or trade. However, there is a conflict for the People of the Book as artists. The commandment *"Thou shalt not make unto thee any graven image, or any likeness* of anything *that is in heaven above, or that is in the earth beneath, or that is in the water under the earth"* (Exodus 20:4) clearly states an artistic dilemma.

A history that, with its prologue, stretches over nearly four thousand years, would not have been possible for all its people without some compromise and interpretation. Thus, a group of Jewish people have found some way to live an observant life and a creative one at the same time. It is by regarding the Jews as a flexible people that we can avoid the error of thinking that, with independence and geographical unity lost, the Jews became only a religious unity. We must remember that the Jews were governed by a religion peculiarly suited to their condition. It is for this reason that over the years Jews have been identifiable as Jews, from China to the Atlantic, both as Jews in a religious sense and also as an integral part of the many different civilizations and cultures of their adopted lands. This dualism was analyzed and considered during early thought about Israel's need for education, and it remains a subject of utmost concern both to Israel's people and government.

As early as 1906 a school of arts and crafts had begun. The Bezalel School of Arts and Crafts was founded by Professor Boris Schatz to teach and maintain the connection between the "love of handwork" and the Jewish people. He considered Bezalel's goal not only the promotion and presentation of Israel's art but the creation of original

28   Bezalel metalworking class (c. 1910)

29   Map of how the Jews traveled to and arrived in Israel

28

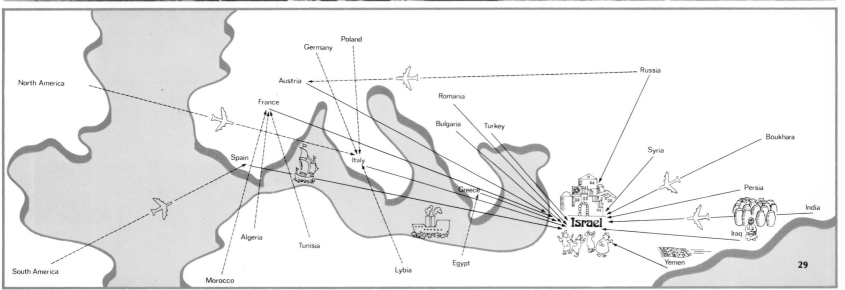

North America

Germany Poland

Austria Russia

France Romania

Spain Bulgaria Turkey

Italy Syria Boukhara

Greece Persia

Algeria India

Tunisia Iraq

Morocco Lybia Egypt Yemen

South America

29

Legend: ----------- not direct route

——————— direct route

art. Indeed, the products of Bezalel became well known to Jews and others interested in education, art, and crafts throughout the world.

Bezalel struggled for its existence for many years until, because of lack of funds, it was closed in 1928. In 1935 the painter Joseph Budko, assisted by teachers and artists who immigrated from Central Europe, succeeded in reopening the school. The school has offered courses in all crafts areas, and its alumni include Israel's finest artisans. Most of the craftsmen represented in this book are graduates of Bezalel. In 1969 Bezalel was raised to the status of Academy of Arts and Design, and it is now recognized as the main educational institution of crafts in Israel.

The faculty of Bezalel includes teachers from all over the world. These teachers are craftsmen themselves and lecture and demonstrate only a day or two a week. This experimental philosophy of education lends itself to satisfying the hunger of the budding craftsman. It provides the opportunity for him to experience many techniques, thoughts, ideas, and cultures and then form his own statements. Bezalel is at the center of Jerusalem and therefore has the distinction of having a perfect setting for such a unique undertaking.

30 Bezalel lithographic class (c. 1910)

31 Bezalel School of Arts and Crafts (c. 1910)

31

33

32 Bezalel ceramic department (c. 1972)
Students' work

33 Bezalel ceramic department (c. 1972)
Students' work

34 Bezalel ceramic department (c. 1972)
Students' work

35 Bezalel ceramic department (c. 1972)
Students' work

36 Bezalel ceramic department (c. 1972)
Students' work

34

35

36

AND SHE DECKED HERSELF

...ותעד נזמה וחליתה...

WITH HER EARRINGS

AND HER JEWELS. HOSEA 2:15

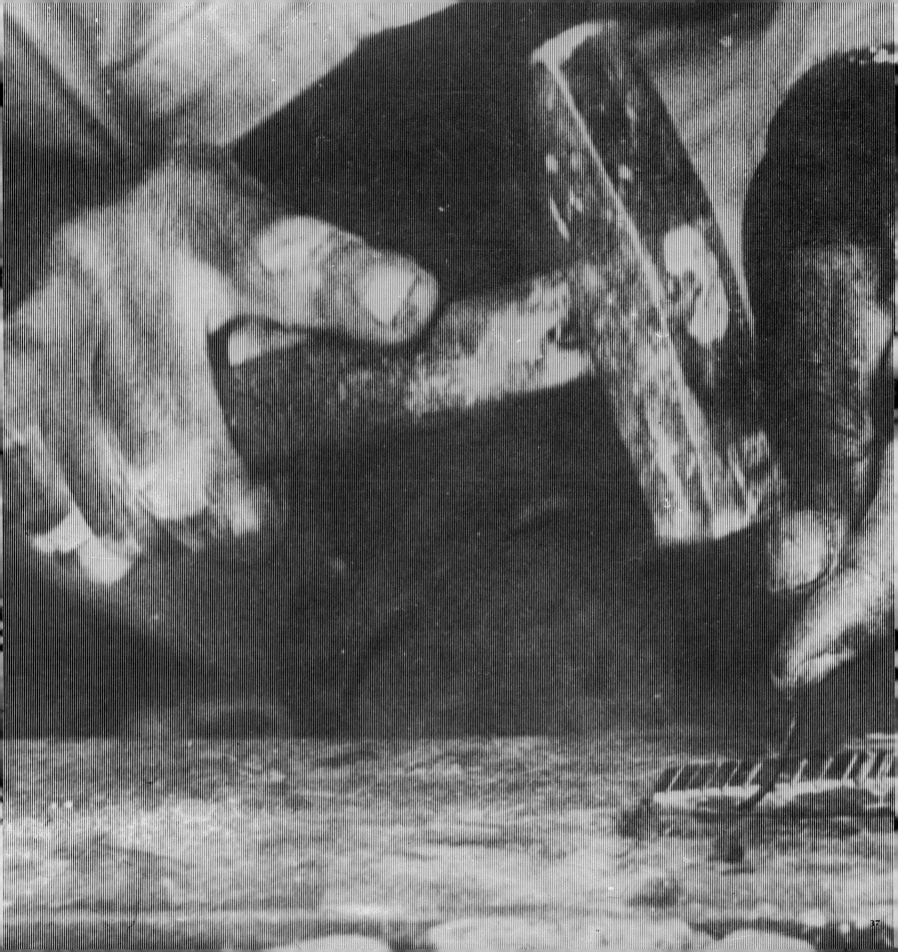

To many people, Israeli jewelry means Yemenite jewelry, and this is not surprising. The immigration of thousands of Yemenite Jews brought with it a myriad of crafts. Jewelry was the major contribution among this wealth of ideas and skills.

Yemenite jewelry is not unlike that of other Middle Eastern countries in outward appearance. It resembles crafts from the part of the world that has surrounded it for centuries. The methods of work were probably learned through the exchange of ideas with Indian merchants, or perhaps resulted from the wish of an Arab sheikh for a jewel to please his favorite of the harem.

The "magic carpet"* that transported Yemenite craftsmen to Israel did more than move them from one country to another; it became the vehicle for the growth of a new industry. By acquiring the skills of the European gem merchant and western technical ability, the Yemenite craftsman, who was in many ways a tenth-century artisan, became the spearhead of a twenty-first-century product. In one generation the jewelry of Israel has moved into world competition and has reached remarkable heights and distinction.

The forming, melting, molding, shaping, stretching, and finishing of such metals as silver or gold are best left in the hands of a supreme craftsman for the creation of a masterpiece. Only after years of work and effort does he learn the mysteries of the transformation of metal into a ring, chalice, or other form. Once the craftsman has met this challenge, he determines how each problem is solved and how the final piece is executed. Precious jewels add to the highlights of metalwork and impart a touch of color or a sign of wealth. The fusing of the pale luster and soft, melodious tones gives to those who look upon these works an appreciation of the achievements of traditional

* The airplanes that flew many missions to evacuate all Jews from Yemen and take them to Israel in 1967 must indeed have seemed like magic carpets to these unsophisticated people, who lighted fires on board to cook their food while aloft!

4 GOLD AND SILVER

38 Earring of silver and enamel
Made for Maskit
Photo: Ben Lam

39 Setting turquoise stones into a traditional piece of jewelry
Photo: Ben Lam

38

39

craftsmanship.

Pride in the centuries of old traditions, integrity, and fine workmanship all go into the creation of a piece of jewelry that will far exceed in quality and worth the value assessed in weight, size, and quality of the stones. To those who work at crafts for the love of creation, the art of the goldsmith and silversmith exemplifies the skill of the craftsman probably to a greater extent than any other art form of modern Israel. The traditional methods of design and work are never static. Fine craftsmanship, rooted in tradition, is combined with original design, complex methods of work, and valuable materials to create jewelry of lasting significance.

Before the hallmark is affixed to a piece of jewelry, bowl, or other craft object, the imprint of its creator is already upon it. Each object must stand alone and contribute its voice to the voices of the crafts of other lands and also enrich the surroundings of Israel. It must not be out of place, yet it must be outstanding; it must blend with the wearer and landscape and still be easily identified. All these criteria are met and mastered by the jewelers of Israel.

40 Silver cast necklace
Made by Mimi Rabinovitz
Photo: Ben Lam

41 Silver necklace with ancient Roman glass
Made by Haim David
Photo: Ben Lam

42 Silver and bead necklace
Made by Mimi Rabinovitz
Photo: Ben Lam

43 Silver necklace with ancient Roman glass
Made for Maskit
Photo: Ben Lam

44 Silver earrings found in "The Cave of Letters"
Made during Bar Kokhba period
(132–135 C.E.)
Photo: David Harris
Courtesy: Yigael Yadin

45 Silver necklace
Made for Maskit, using the idea of the earrings found in "The Cave of Letters"
Photo: Ben Lam

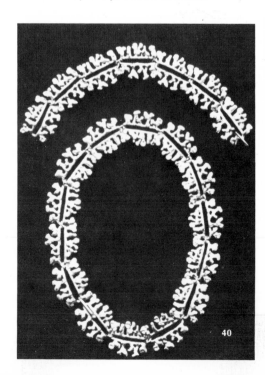

40

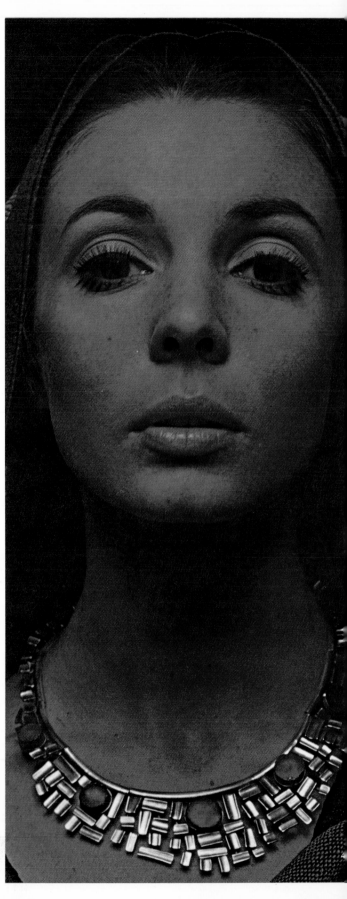

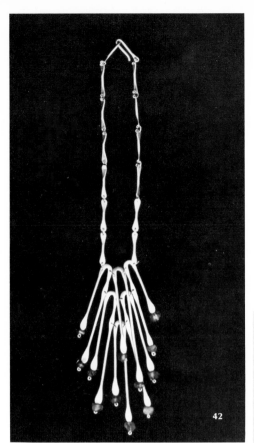

42

43

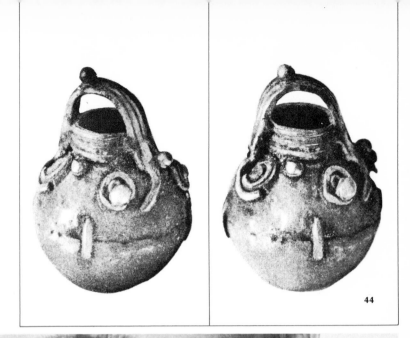

44

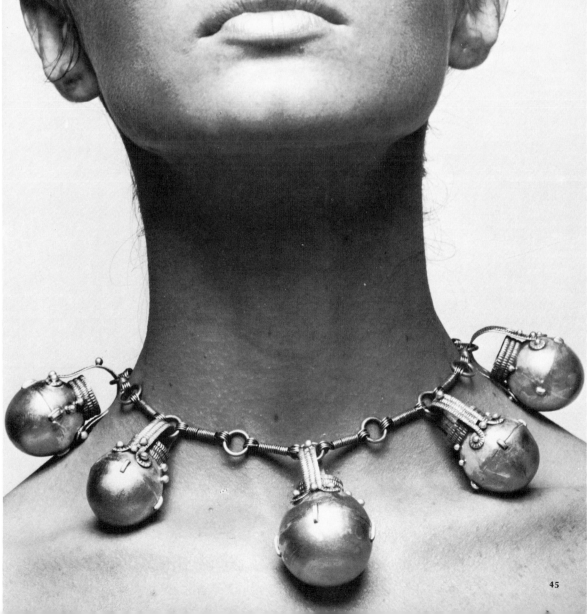

45

46 Gold pin
Made by Bianca Eshel

47 Gold pin
Made by Bianca Eshel

48 Gold pin
Made by Bianca Eshel

49 Gold pin
Made by Bianca Eshel

50 Gold pin
Made by Bianca Eshel

51 Gold pin
Made by Bianca Eshel

52 Gold pin
Made by Bianca Eshel

53 Gold ring
Turquoise, jade, coral
Made by Bianca Eshel

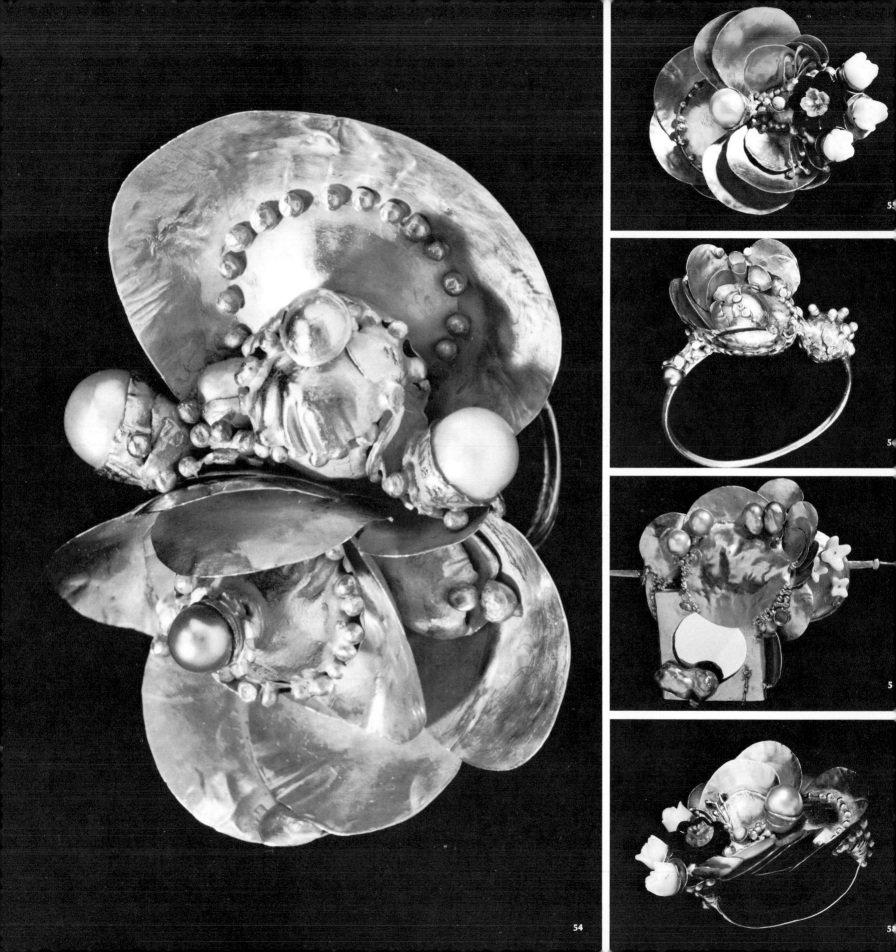

54

55

5

5

5

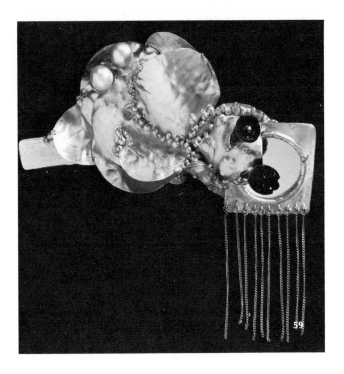

54   **Gold ring**
Made by Bianca Eshel

55   **Gold pin**
Made by Bianca Eshel

56   **Gold ring**
Made by Bianca Eshel
Photo: Benny Badarshi

57   **Gold pin**
Made by Bianca Eshel

58   **Gold ring**
Made by Bianca Eshel
Photo: Benny Badarshi

59   **Gold ring**
Made by Bianca Eshel
Photo: Benny Badarshi

60

61

62

63

60 **18-carat gold ring set with diamonds and pearls**
Made by Arieh Ophir

61 **18-carat gold ring set with diamonds**
Made by Arieh Ophir

62 **18-carat gold ring set with diamonds**
Made by Arieh Ophir

63 **18-carat gold ring set with diamonds and black pearls**
Made by Arieh Ophir

64 **18-carat gold ring with jag**
Made by Arieh Ophir

65 **18-carat gold ring set with diamonds**
Made by Arieh Ophir

Photo: R. Milon

66 **18-carat gold ring set with diamonds and black pearls**
Made by Arieh Ophir

64

65

66

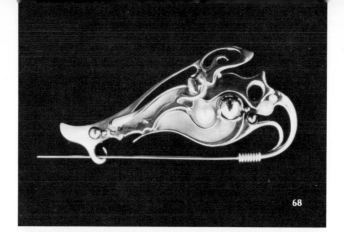

68

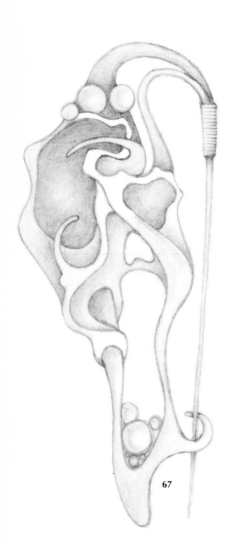

67

69

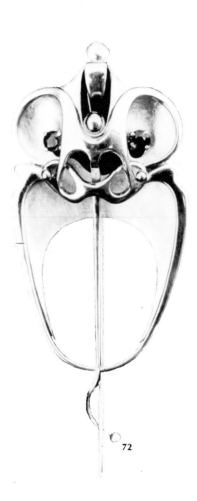

72

70

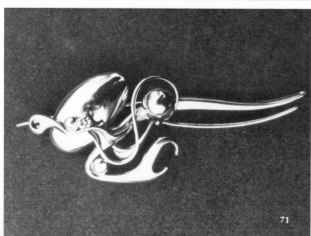

71

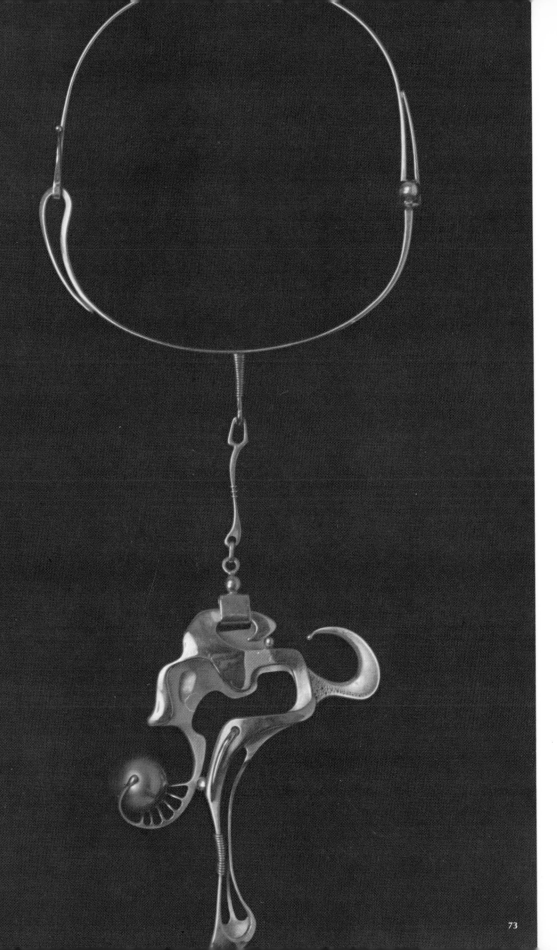

67 **Original drawing**
By Amitai Kav

68 **Gold pin with black and white pearls**
Made by Amitai Kav

69 **Gold pin**
Made by Amitai Kav

70 **Gold pin with pearls**
Made by Amitai Kav

71 **Gold pin**
Made by Amitai Kav

72 **Gold pin with sapphires**
Made by Amitai Kav

73 **Gold neck piece**
Made by Amitai Kav
Photo: Ephraim Kidron

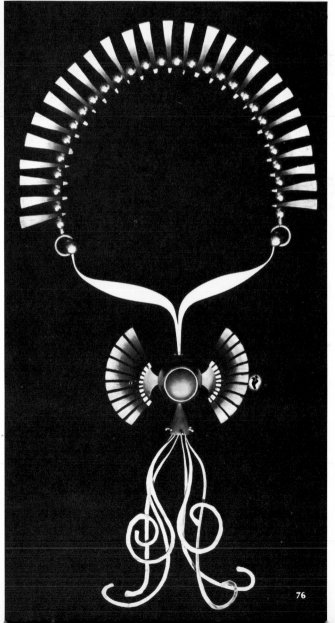

74   Gold ring (cast)
Made by Maury Golan

75   Silver pin, topaz crystal
Made by Maury Golan

76   Pendant
Gold-plated silver, moonstone
Made by Maury Golan

77   Traditional silver neck piece
Opens to become a container
Made for Maskit

78   Traditional Yemenite neck piece
Silver and coral
Photo: Ben Lam

77

78

79 Silver neck piece
Enamel and semiprecious stones
From Morocco
Photo: Zev Radovan
Courtesy: The Israel Museum, Jerusalem

80 Men's festive belts
Inlaid, carved, enameled, niello,
turquoise stones in setting
From Bukhara
Courtesy: The Israel Museum, Jerusalem

81 Silver bracelet
Original design from Yemen
Made for Maskit
Photo: Ruben Marton

82 Silver pins
Enamel and semiprecious stones
From Morocco
Photo: Zev Radovan
Courtesy: The Israel Museum, Jerusalem

83 Woman's decoration for the chest
Silver
From Morocco
Photo: Zev Radovan
Courtesy: The Israel Museum, Jerusalem

84 Silver earrings
Original design from Tunisia
Photo: Zev Radovan
Courtesy: The Israel Museum, Jerusalem

79

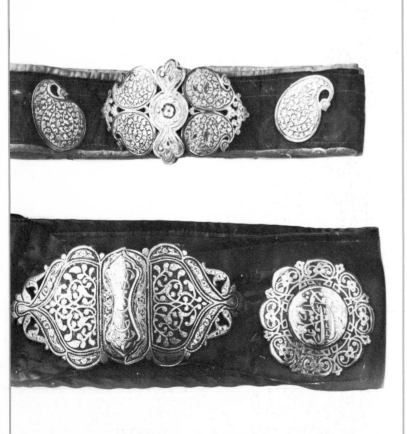

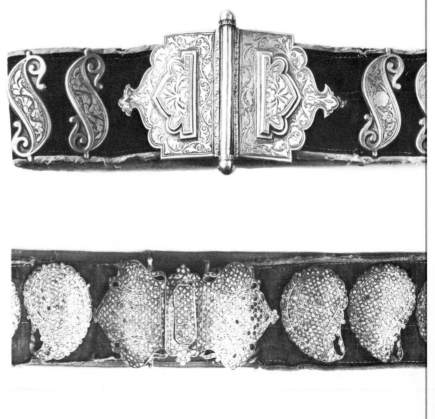

80

81

82

83

84

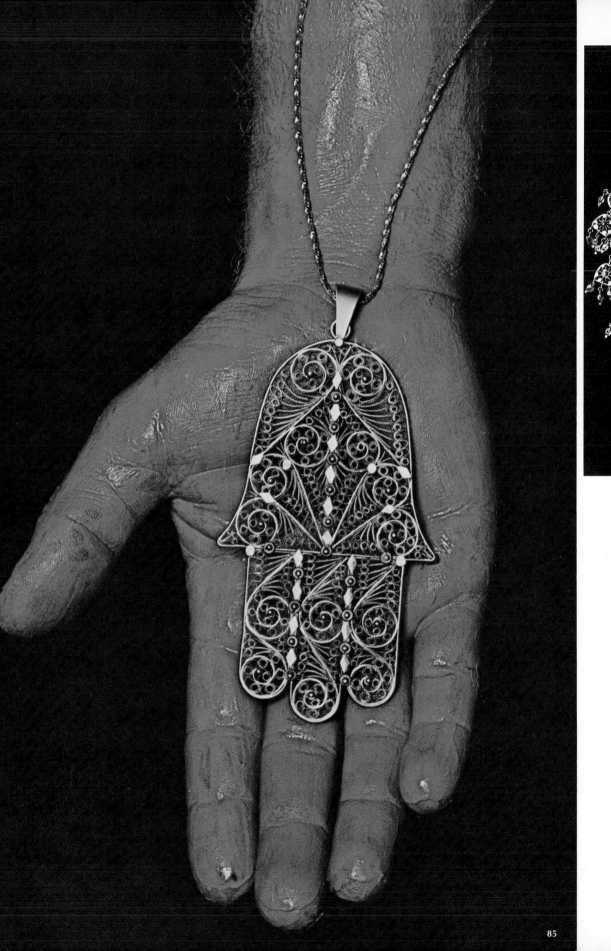

85   Traditional Algerian filigree hamsa
Used against the "Evil Eye"
Gold, designed by Tweto for Maskit
Photo: Ephraim Kidron

86   Traditional Yemenite necklace
Silver
Photo: Ephraim Kidron

87   Traditional Yemenite filigree choshin necklace
Silver, made for Maskit
Photo: Ephraim Kidron

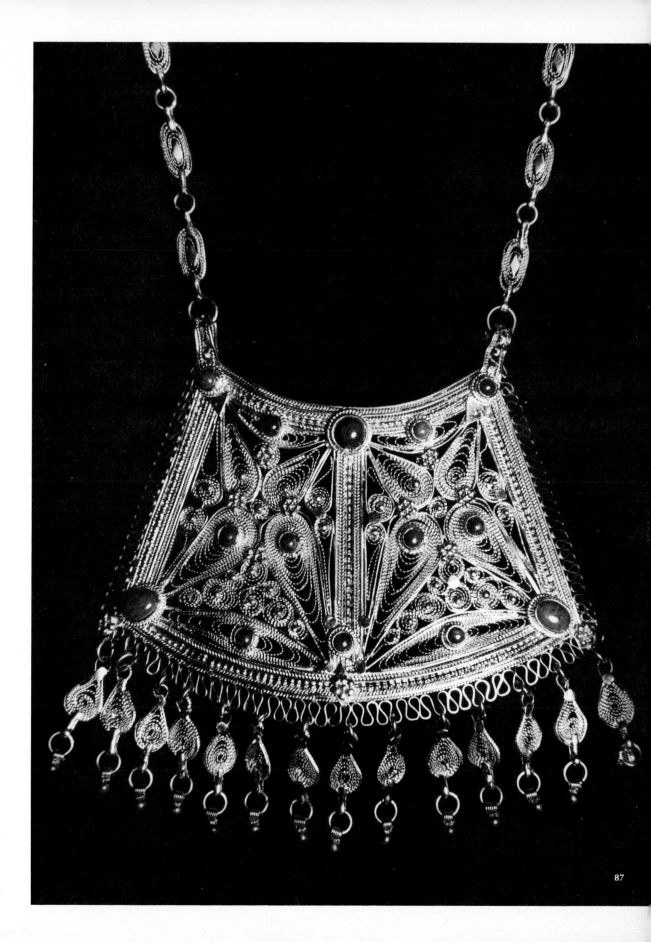

87

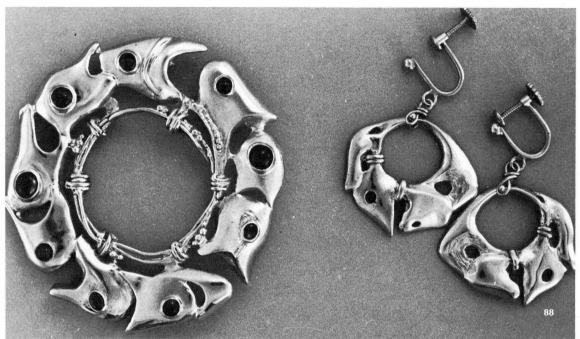

91

88   Silver pin and earrings
Made by Hannah Behar

89   Gold ring
Made by Hannah Behar

90   Silver brooch and earrings with tourmaline stones
Made by Hannah Behar
Photo: Nat Suffrin

91   Bracelets of amber and silver
Made by Hannah Behar
Photo: Yaccov Panet

92   18-carat gold pin with baroque pearls and amethyst stones
Made by Hannah Behar
Photo: Benny Kalinsky

93   18-carat gold pin with baroque pearls
Made by Hannah Behar
Photo: Benny Kalinsky

94   18-carat gold pin with pearls
Made by Hannah Behar
Photo: Benny Kalinsky

95   Gold necklace with fresh-water pearls
Made by Hannah Behar
Photo: Ephraim Kidron

96   Neck piece
Silver and wool
Made by Hannah Behar
Photo: Nat Suffrin

97   Silver necklace
Made by Hannah Behar
Photo: Nat Suffrin

98   Neck piece
Silver and wool
Made by Hannah Behar
Photo: Nat Suffrin

99   Neck piece
Silver and wool
Made by Hannah Behar
Photo: Nat Suffrin

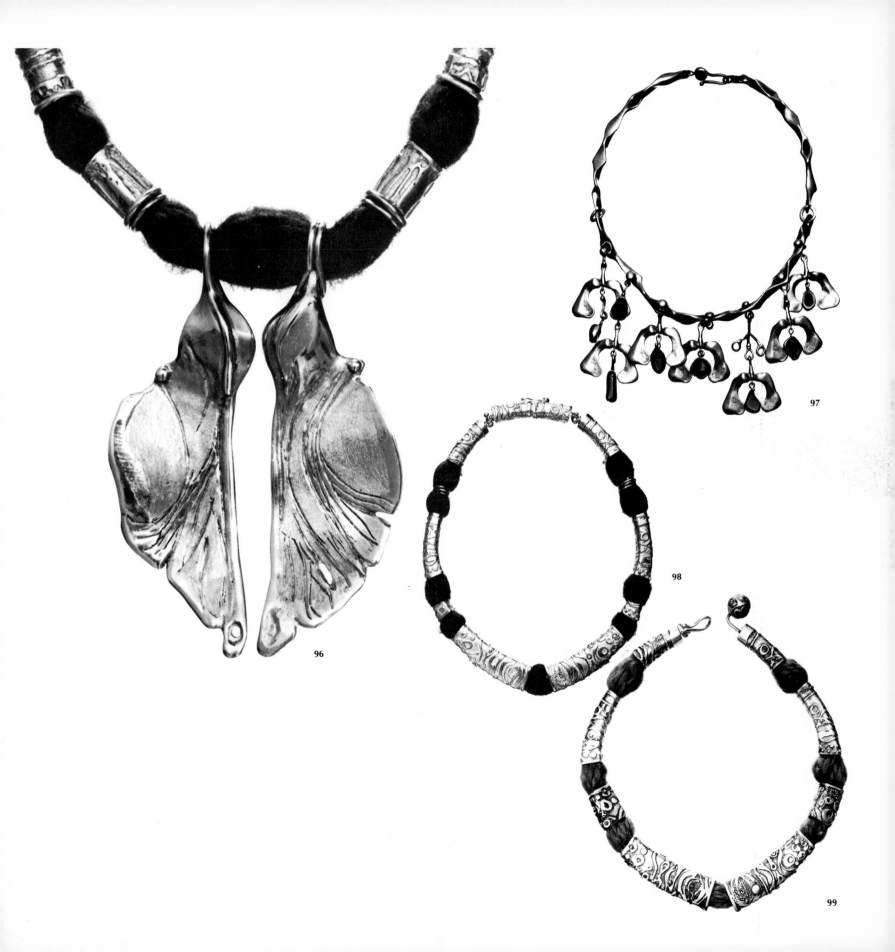

96

97

98

99

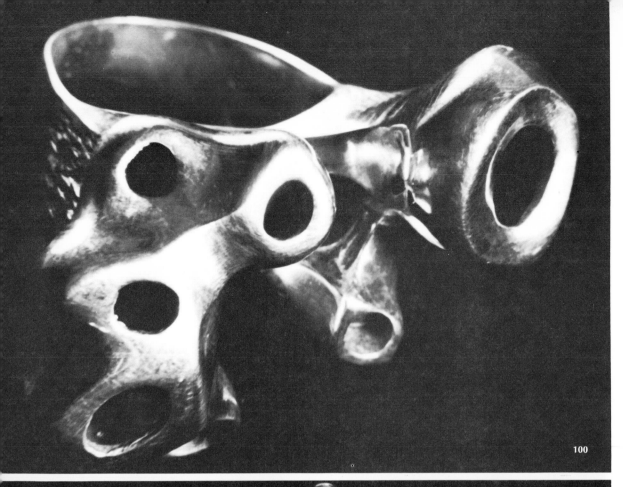

100 Silver ring
Made by Ruth and Ed Sernoff
Photo: Ephraim Kidron

101 Silver pin
Made by Ruth and Ed Sernoff
Photo: Ephraim Kidron

102 Silver necklace
Made by Ruth and Ed Sernoff
Photo: Ephraim Kidron

103 Original drawing for necklace
Made by Leon Israel

104 Original design for hair comb
Made by Leon Israel

105 Gold necklace
With diamond, opals, pearls
Made by Leon Israel
Photo: Ephraim Kidron

106 Gold hair comb
Diamonds, jade, pearls
Made by Leon Israel

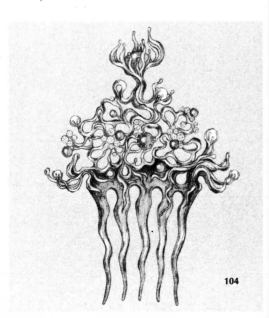

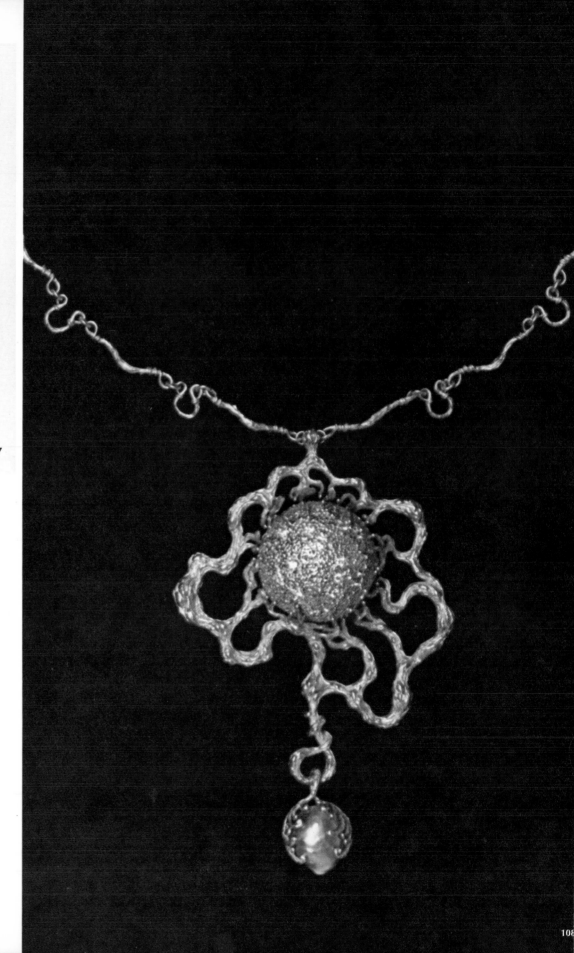

107 Original design for neck piece
Made by Leon Israel

**108 White and yellow gold
neck piece**
Set with diamonds and fresh-water pearls
Made by Leon Israel
Photo: Ephraim Kidron

109 Silver neck piece
Agate and pearls
Made by GERA

110

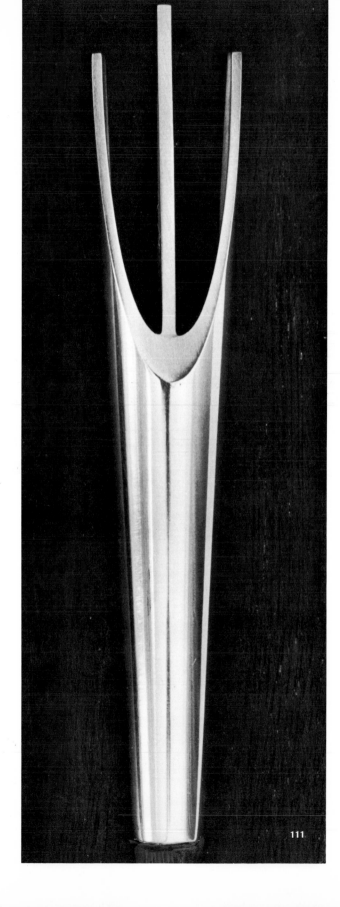

111

112

110   Silver mezuza
Religious object
Made by Maury Golan
Photo: Ephraim Kidron

111   Silver mezuza
Religious object
Made by David Gumbel
Photo: R. Milon

112   Silver Passover seder plate
Religious object
Made by Zelig Sigal

113   Silver Passover set
Religious object
Made by Zelig Sigal

113

114

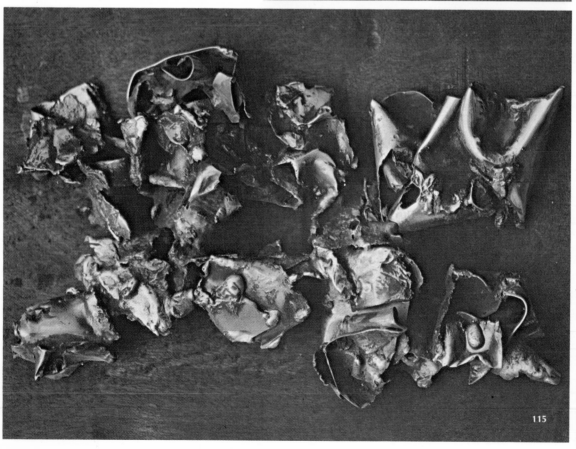

115

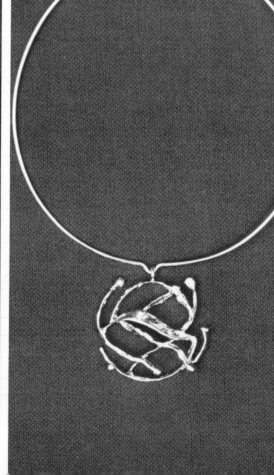

114 14-carat gold bracelet
Made by Kurt Pfeffermann
Photo: Sadeh

115 Welded brass wall plaque
Made by Kurt Pfeffermann
Photo: Sadeh

116 14-carat gold pendant
Made by Kurt Pfeffermann
Photo: Sadeh

117 Brass candlestick
Made by Kurt Pfeffermann
Photo: Sadeh

118 14-carat gold pendant
Made by Kurt Pfeffermann
Photo: Sadeh

119 Channukah candelabrum, welded brass
Made by Kurt Pfeffermann
Photo: Sadeh

120 Wall plaque, welded brass
Made by Kurt Pfeffermann
Photo: Sadeh

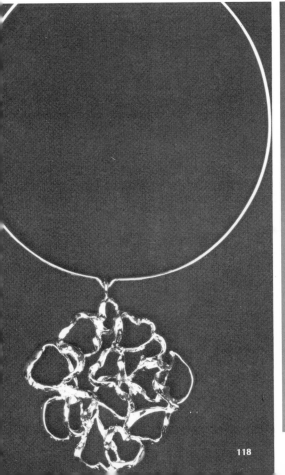

118

117

119

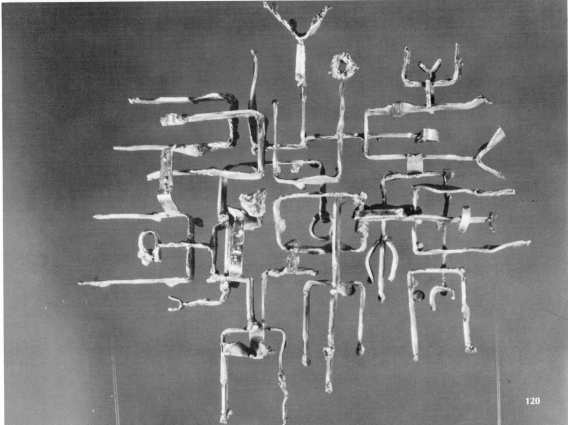

120

121

122

123

124

121 Silver Passover seder plate
Religious object
Made by Menahem Berman

122 Silver service set, flatware
Designed for Rosenthal Studio Line (in production)
Made by Menahem Berman

123 Elijah cup
Silver with amethyst and hand-blown glass
30 cm. high
Made by Menahem Berman

124 Etrog container
Silver with amethyst (lost-wax method)
Religious object
20 cm. high
Made by Menahem Berman

125 Silver cup
30 cm. high
Made by Menahem Berman
Photo: Wilburt Feinberg

126 Brass Channukah candelabrum with wengé wood base
Designed for Chaim Paz Ltd. by Menahem Berman
30 cm. high
Photo: Wilburt Feinberg

125

126

127

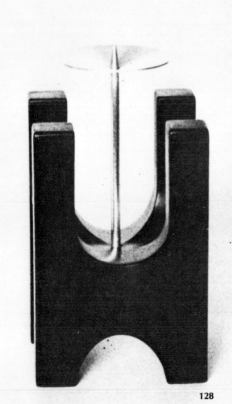

128

127 Channukah lamp
Religious object
Ebony wood with sterling silver
Made by Noam Harkabi
Photo: Norbert

128 Candle holder
Ebony and silver
Made by Noam Harkabi

129 Silver chalice
(Electroforming process)
20 cm. high
Made by Maury Golan

130 Gold perfume phial
(Electroforming process)
Made by Maury Golan

131

131 Seder plate
Religious object used for Passover
Sterling silver
Made by Arieh Ophir
Photo: R. Milon

132 Etrog box
Religious object
Sterling silver
Made by Arieh Ophir
Photo: R. Milon

133 Kidush (Prayer cup)
Religious object
Sterling silver
Made by Arieh Ophir
Photo: R. Milon

134 Kidush (Prayer cup)
Religious object
Sterling silver
Made by Arieh Ophir
Photo: R. Milon

135 Elijah cup
Sterling silver
Made by Arieh Ophir
Photo: R. Milon

136 Kidush (Prayer cup)
Religious object
Sterling silver
Made by Arieh Ophir
Photo: R. Milon

13

133

134

135

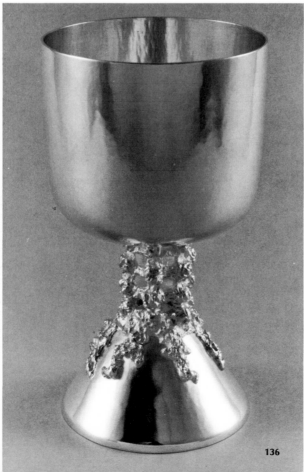

136

AN ALTAR OF EARTH THOU SHALT

מזבח אדמה תעשה־לי וזבחת

MAKE UNTO ME, AND SHALT

עליו את־עלתיך ואת־שלמיך

SACRIFICE THEREON THY

את־צאנך ואת־בקרך בכל־המקום

BURNT-OFFERINGS, AND THY

אשר אזכיר את־שמי

PEACE-OFFERINGS, THY SHEEP, AND

אבוא אליך וברכתיך:

THINE OXEN: IN EVERY PLACE

WHERE I CAUSE MY NAME TO BE

MENTIONED I WILL COME UNTO

THEE, AND BLESS THEE. EXODUS 20:21

137 "Potter in Gaza"
Working in underground caves
Photo. Wilburt Feinberg

Clay and sand are found in all parts of our country, but only a potter can awaken the hidden beauty in them. The basic methods of working clay are the same all over the world. There have been ceramic craftsmen for ten thousand years of archaeological history; pottery is one of mankind's first crafts. Clay, more than any other medium, can reflect the thoughts and movements of the creator. He breathes life into the plastic earth and forms it into an expression of himself and his world.

The Israeli potter finds his medium deep in the soil around Jerusalem, Bethlehem, and the arid Negev. At times the craftsman introduces foreign elements into native clay bodies and uses clay from other parts of the world. This mixture is familiar to Israeli crafts, and the diversified sources of materials and methods stimutate the craftsman's imagination.

To find a potter at work, we might have to enter a nineteenth-century Arab house built with walls one meter thick. The thick walls are needed to hold moisture within the house and to provide a shelter from the oppressive hot, dry wind of the desert. The rapid evaporation caused by these winds can ruin the most prized works. The kiln is often built from fire brick that is taken from ancient ovens that have proven their long years' worth and add to the mellow fire that bakes the dust into permanence.

With a deep love of clay, of form, texture, splash of vivid color, the potter learns his craft. Once he has developed and controlled the techniques, he has within his hands the ability to create a mirror of his people. What could be more rewarding than to form a colorless, lifeless lump of dust into warmth and life?

5 CLAY AND EARTH

138 Title page
Hebrew and English text (Exodus 20:24)
Printed on black paper with metallic
gold and silver ink

139 Detail of No. 140 (ceramic wall)
Made by Gedula Ogen

מזבח אדמה תעשה לי
וזבחת עליו את עלתיך
בכל המקום אשר אזכיר
את שמי
אבוא אליך וברכתיך

שמות: כ: כא

AN ALTAR OF EARTH THOU SHALT MAKE
UNTO ME, AND SHALT SACRIFICE THEREON
THY BURNT OFFERINGS, AND THY PEACE
OFFERINGS, THY SHEEP AND THINE OXEN:
IN ALL PLACES WHERE I RECORD MY NAME
I WILL COME UNTO THEE, AND I WILL
BLESS THEE.

EXODUS: 20:24

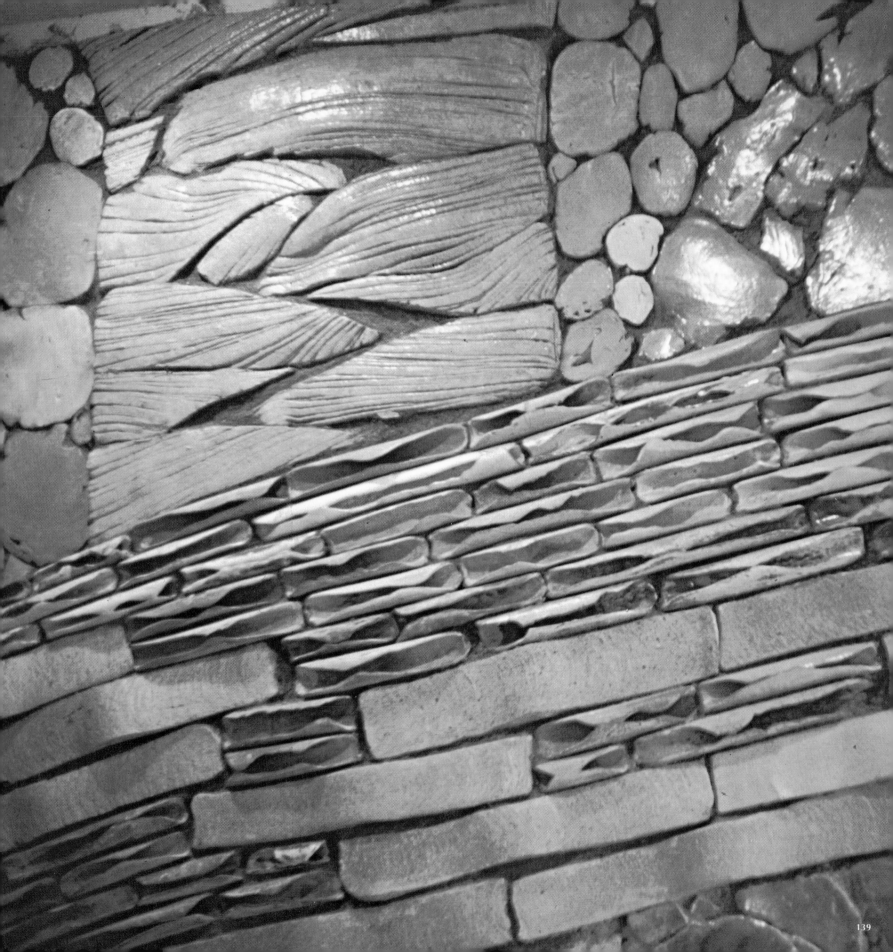

140

140 Ceramic wall
Made by Gedula Ogen

141 Ceramic wall
Made by Gedula Ogen
Photo: S. J. Schweig

142 Detail of large wall
Made by Gedula Ogen

143 Detail of large wall
Made by Gedula Ogen

144 "An altar of earth"
Made by Gedula Ogen

145   "Trees"
Made by Gedula Ogen
Photo: S. J. Schweig

146   Detail of large wall
Made by Daniel Nahum

146

147

148

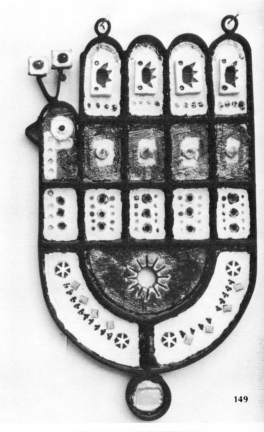

149

147 **"King and Queen"**
Made by Daniel Nahum

148 **"David and his Harp"**
Made by Daniel Nahum

149 **Hamsa (against the evil eye)**
Ceramic wall piece
Made by Daniel Nahum

150 **Hamsa (against the evil eye)**
Ceramic wall piece
Made by Daniel Nahum

151 **Hamsa (against the evil eye)**
Ceramic wall piece
Made by Daniel Nahum

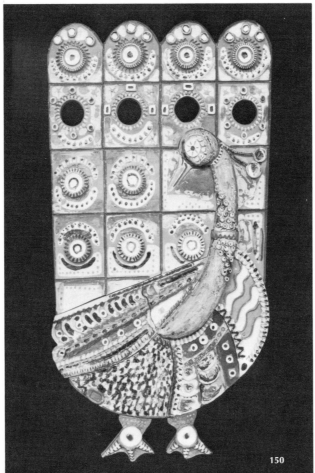

150

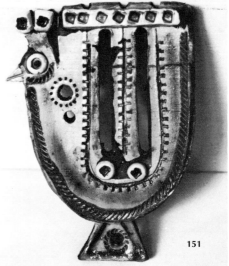

151

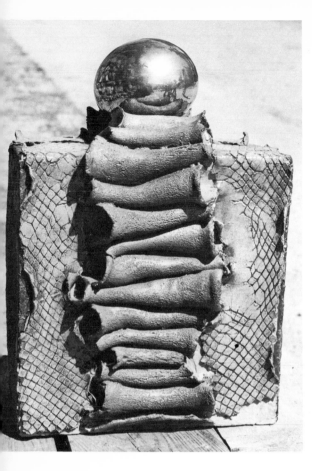

152

153

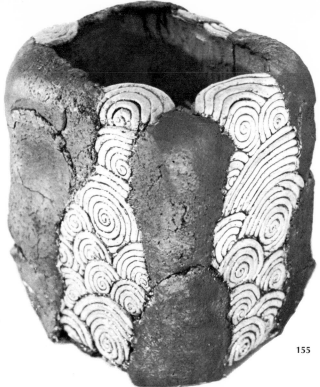

155

156

157

152   Stoneware cube with gold ball
37 cm. high
Made by Lidia Zavadsky

153   Black and white sculpture-stoneware
100 cm. high
Made by Lidia Zavadsky

154   Stoneware cube
Made by Lidia Zavadsky
50 cm. high

155   Stoneware vase
40 × 40 cm, height 55 cm.
Made by Lidia Zavadsky

156   Stoneware vase
40 × 40 cm., height 110 cm.
Made by Lidia Zavadsky

157   Stoneware vase
30 × 30 cm., height 75 cm.
Made by Lidia Zavadsky

158

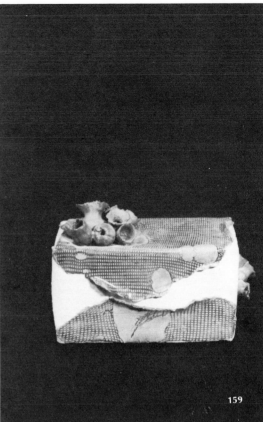

159

160

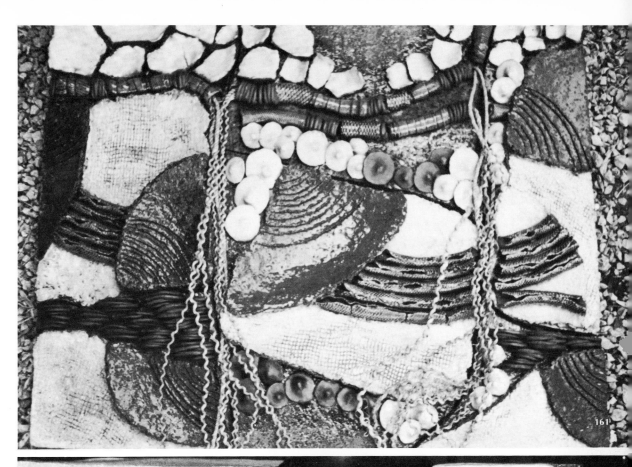

158 **Stoneware cube with gold ball**
50 cm. high
Made by Lidia Zavadsky
Photo: Wilburt Feinberg

159 **Stoneware cube**
30 cm. high
Made by Lidia Zavadsky
Photo: Wilburt Feinberg

160 **White cube with cobalt glass**
45 cm. high
Made by Lidia Zavadsky

161 **"Landscape" stoneware relief**
100 cm. x 80 cm.
Made by Lidia Zavadsky

162 **Composition stoneware cube with red cord**
Made by Lidia Zavadsky

162

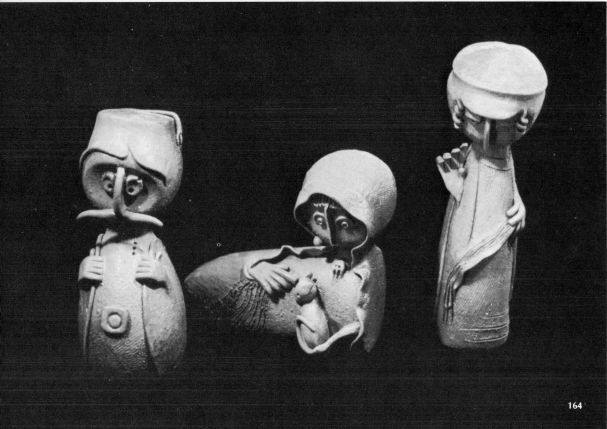

163 Stoneware "Face"
Made by Marek Gezola
Photo: Wilburt Feinberg

164 Stoneware "People"
Made by Marek Gezola
Photo: Wilburt Feinberg

165 Stoneware figure
Made by Marek Gezola
Photo: Asher Molet

166 Stoneware figures
Made by Marek Gezola
Photo: Asher Molet

167 Stoneware figures
Made by Marek Gezola
Photo: Asher Molet

168 Stoneware family
Made by Marek Gezola
Photo: Asher Molet

169 Stoneware figures
Made by Marek Gezola
Photo: Asher Molet

170 "Figure with vase"
Stoneware
Made by Marek Gezola
Photo: Asher Molet

165

166

167

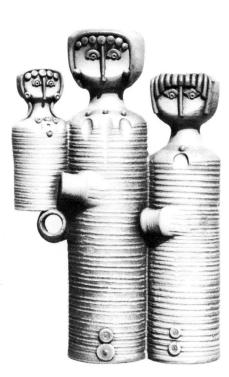

168

169

170

171

172

171   Stoneware Gremlins
Made by Marek Gezola
Photo: Asher Molet

172   Sculpture stoneware
Made by Marek Gezola
Photo: Asher Molet

173   Bottles
Made by Miriam Nueman
Photo: Asher Molet

174   "Torn pots"
Stoneware
Made by Marek Gezola
Photo: Asher Molet

173

174

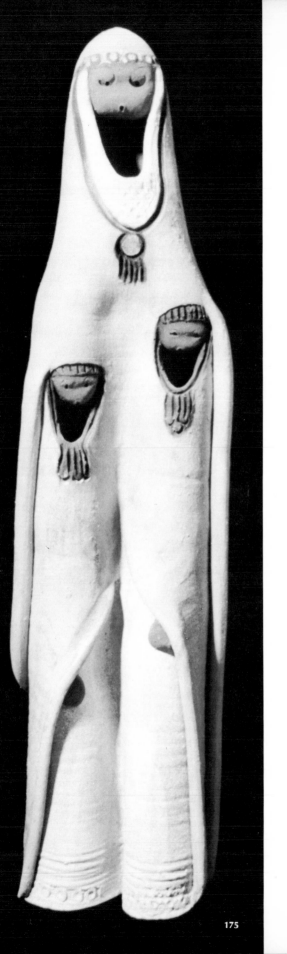

175   Stoneware "Bedouin and Children"
Made by David Calderon
Photo: Wilburt Feinberg

176   Stoneware figure
Made by Rachel Berenson
Photo: Wilburt Feinberg

177   Stoneware figure
Made by Miriam Magnes
Photo: Wilburt Feinberg

178

179

180

182

183

178   **Stoneware sculpture "From the Desert"**
120 cm. high
Made by Niomi and Nora

179   **Stoneware sculpture "Pillars"**
Made by Niomi and Nora

180   **Detail of stoneware wall**
Made by Niomi and Nora

181   **Stoneware sculpture**
Made by Niomi and Nora

182   **Stoneware sculpture**
Made by Niomi and Nora

183   **Stoneware candelabra sculpture**
Fired at 1060°F
Made by Niomi and Nora

184 Sculpture brick
For walls and room dividers
Designed for industry
Made by Hanna Charag-Zuntz

185 Part of wall
Made of wheel-thrown earthenware
bowls, majolica glazes
Made by Hanna Charag-Zuntz

186 Lamp base
Rough fired clay, slip glaze
52 cm. high
Made by Hanna Charag-Zuntz
Photo: Nativ Israel

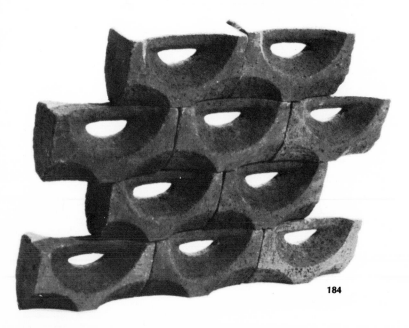

184

186

185

187 Left bottle (tall, slim)
Stoneware, Negev clay, buff color
35 cm. high
Photo: Sadeh

Right bottle (short, squat)
Fine earthenware with terra sigillate
28 cm. high
Deep blue, brown, black
Made by Hanna Charag-Zuntz

188 Lamp base
50 cm. high
Made by Hanna Charag-Zuntz

189 A-E Five earthenware vases
Made by Hanna Charag-Zuntz

187

188

189A

189B

189C

189D

189E

190

191

192

190 "Potter in Gaza"
Working in underground caves
Photo: Wilburt Feinberg

191 Kfar Samir pottery works
Haifa beach, Atallah family's courtyard
Photo: Yolanda Zuerich

192 Kfar Samir pottery works
Haifa beach, Atallah family
Part-drying of half-finished big drums.
The moist rags placed in the base of the
unfinished drums slow the drying
process.
Photo: Yolanda Zuerich

193 "Cousin"
Earthenware
Made by Edith Ady
60 cm. high

194 Stoneware sculpture
Made by Edith Ady
75 cm. high
Photo: Nir Bareket

193

194

AND THOU SHALT MAKE A VEIL OF

ועשית פרכת תכלת וארגמן ותולעת שני . . .

BLUE, AND PURPLE, AND SCARLET,

AND FINE TWINED LINEN . . . . EXODUS 26:31

A GOLDEN BELL AND A

פעמן זהב ורמון פעמן זהב ורמון

POMEGRANATE, A GOLDEN BELL

על־שולי המעיל סביב:

AND A POMEGRANATE,

UPON THE HEM OF THE ROBE

ROUND ABOUT. EXODUS 28:34

195 Hana Kralova at work
Bobbin lace work

6 THREADS AND FIBERS

Camel, goat, sheep, and horse hair, cotton, gold, silver, wood, reed, rayon, nylon, and other fibers—to weave, sew, embroider. These may be transformed into a cover for a tent, a cloak against the cold desert night, a shade from the burning sun, a dress for the most chic, a simple throw to warm the home, a dash of color upon a floor, or a work of magnificent dimensions upon a wall.

Today Israel uses her ancient skills in combination with new ones to produce textures of lasting beauty. Weaving, rug making, embroidery, lace work, and a host of other textile techniques are part of the treasure of knowledge brought to Israel by its newcomers. A growing industry of woven and knotted works has found its place in the Israeli world of crafts.

In our discoveries of the earliest civilizations we find traces of cloth that not only had functional use but were a form of decoration in rather drab surroundings. To distinguish and set apart one's clan or tribe or to introduce unique character into one's household is not a modern idea, and although in the past, as in modern times, a lavish display is frowned upon, subtle works of good taste are now and always have been appreciated.

196

196   Traditional Bethlehem dress
Embroidered with silk thread on cotton and silk material
Photo: Ben Lam

197   Traditional Yemenite embroidery
Photo: Ephraim Kidron

198 Desert coat
Original design by Finny Lietersdorf for Maskit
Inspired by traditional "Abaya" coat of the desert people
Photo: Ben Lam

199 Crochet work
Designed for Maskit by Mitzi Bar-Orian
Photo: Ben Lam

200 Contemporary use of traditional designs
Made for Maskit
Photo: Ben Lam

201 Batik dresses
Designed for Maskit

202 Silk-screened dress
Designed by Ruth Sternshuss
Photo: Ben Lam

200

201

202

203 **Felt appliquéd on coarse linen**
Bible themes
Made by Kopel Gurwin

204 **Felt appliquéd on coarse linen**
Bible themes
Made by Kopel Gurwin

205 **Felt appliquéd on coarse linen**
Bible themes
Made by Kopel Gurwin

206 **Hamsa appliqué**
Made of wool, felt, velvet, and wood
and glass beads
Made by Shulamit Litan

206

207

207 "Sunset" appliqué and stitchery
on wool
Made of velvet, silk, felt, and wooden
beads
Made by Shulamit Litan

208 Detail of patchwork skirt
Cotton, wool, and felt
Made by Shulamit Litan

209 Hand-quilted batik on silk
Quote from Psalms 122:6
"Pray for the peace of Jerusalem:
they shall prosper that love thee."
Made by Shulamit Litan

210 "Industry" appliqué
Made by Shulamit Litan

211 Channukah jars appliqué
Made by Shulamit Litan

208

210

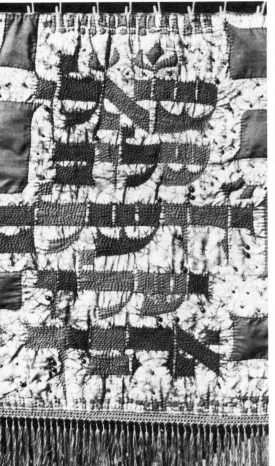

209

211

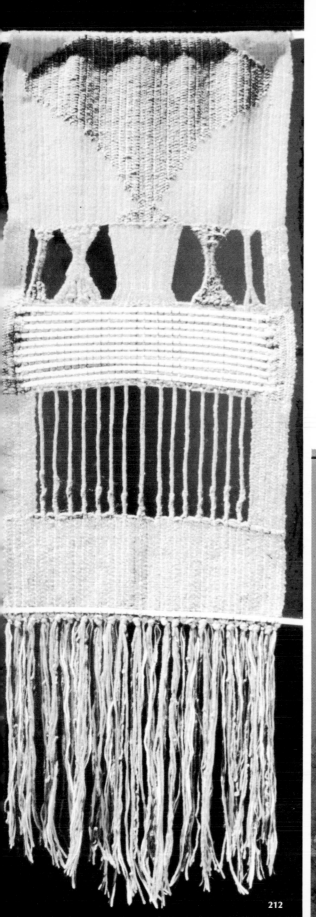

212

212 Wall hanging
Wool and bamboo
Made by Yehudit Katz
Photo: Dalia Amotz

213 Hanging
Wool, synthetic fiber, and metal thread
Made by Yehudit Katz
Photo: Dalia Amotz

214 "Mother and Child"
Bobbin lace work by Hana Kralova

214

215 "The Garden of Eden"
Bobbin lace work by Hana Kralova

216 "In the Clouds"
Bobbin lace work by Hana Kralova

217 "Sunrise"
Bobbin lace work by Hana Kralova

218 "The Camel"
Bobbin lace work by students of Hana Kralova

219 "Cap and Bells"
Bobbin lace work by students of Hana Kralova

220 "The Kid with the Ball"
Bobbin lace work by students of Hana Kralova

221 "Full Moon"
Bobbin lace work by students of Hana Kralova

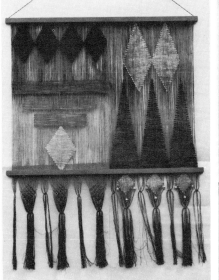

218

219

220

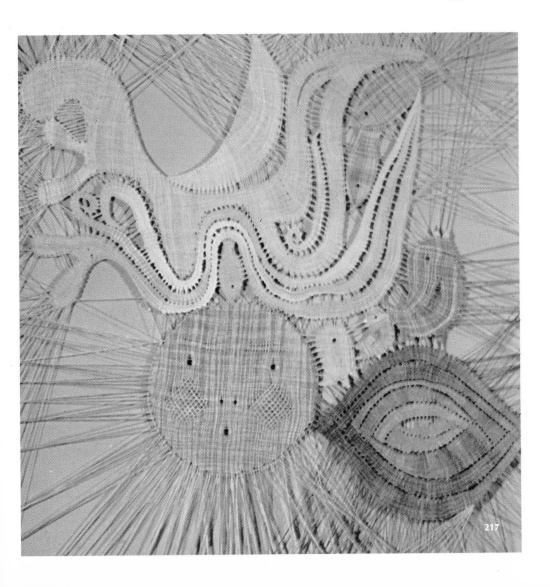

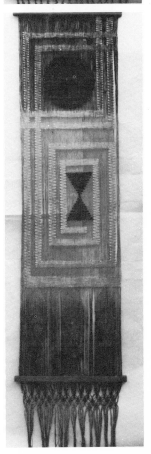

217

221

222

223

222 Spinning the wool
Gaza
Photo: Wilburt Feinberg

223 Bringing wool to be woven after washing in the sea
Gaza rug makers
Photo: Wilburt Feinberg

224 Weaving rugs
Gaza
Photo: Wilburt Feinberg

225 Weaving rugs
Gaza
Photo: Wilburt Feinberg

227

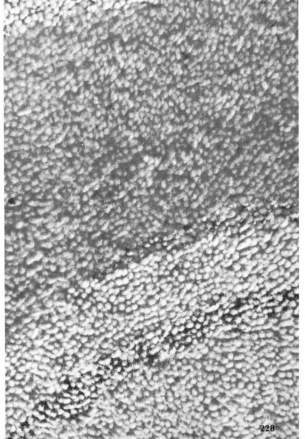

228

226

229

226 Detail of wool rug (pile)
Photo: Wilburt Feinberg

227 Wool rug
Designed for Maskit by Siona Shimshi
Photo: Wilburt Feinberg

228 Detail of wool rug (pile)
Photo: Ephraim Kidron

229 Wool rug
Traditional pattern
Photo: Ephraim Kidron

230 Wool rug
Traditional pattern
Photo: Ephraim Kidron

230

231

232

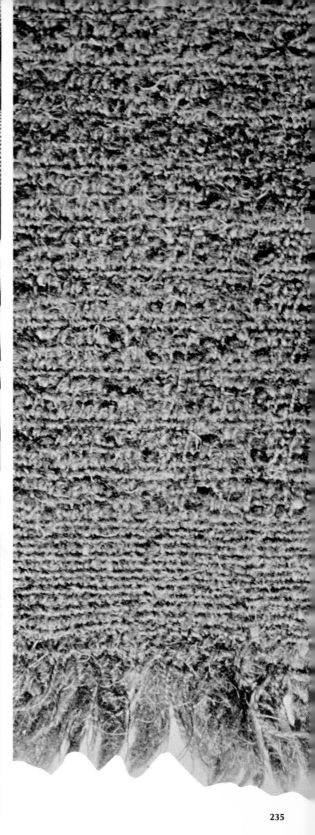

233

234

235

231 Wool rug for the Plaza Hotel, Tel Aviv
Designed by Siona Shimshi for Maskit
Photo: Ephraim Kidron

232 Wool rug
Designed by Erika Kluger
Photo: Ephraim Kidron

233 Handwoven wool
Designed for Maskit by Neora Warshavsky
Photo: Ben Lam

234 Handwoven linen
Designed for Maskit by Neora Warshavsky
Photo: Ben Lam

235 Handwoven Irish wool
Designed for the Irish Handweaving Mill in Ireland by Neora Warshavsky
For upholstery and tweeds
Photo: Yaki Molho

240

241

236 Handwoven Irish wool
Designed for the Irish Handweaving Mill
in Ireland by Neora Warshavsky
For upholstery and tweeds
Photo: Yaki Molho

237 Handwoven Irish wool
Designed for the Irish Handweaving Mill
in Ireland by Neora Warshavsky
For upholstery and tweeds
Photo: Yaki Molho

238 Handwoven Irish wool
Designed for the Irish Handweaving Mill
in Ireland by Neora Warshavsky
For upholstery and tweeds
Photo: Yaki Molho

239 Handwoven upholstery fabric (wool)
Designed for Maskit by Neora
Warshavsky

240 Handwoven drapery linen
Designed for Maskit by Neora
Warshavsky

241 Handwoven cotton
Designed for Maskit by Neora
Warshavsky

242 Handwoven wool for drapery
Designed for Maskit by Neora
Warshavsky
Light upholstery, suiting fabric

243 Heavy handwoven wool tweed
Designed for Maskit by Neora
Warshavsky

242

243

244–254   Samples of textures in handwoven fabrics

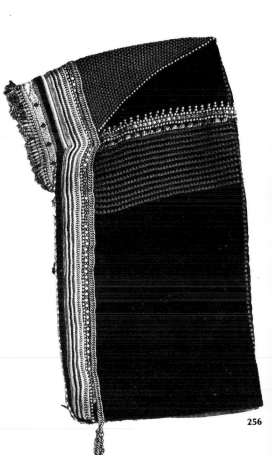

255

256

255 Detail of embroidery on Yemenite traditional dress
Courtesy: The Israel Museum, Jerusalem

256 Traditional Yemenite woman's hat
Courtesy: The Israel Museum, Jerusalem

257 Examples of Yemenite woman's leggings worn for festive occasions
Photo: R. M. Kneller
Courtesy: The Israel Museum, Jerusalem

258 Traditional Yemenite woman's hat for ceremonial wear
Photo: David Harris
Courtesy: The Israel Museum, Jerusalem

259 Detail of Woman's Hat
Silver embroidery on velvet
Courtesy: The Israel Museum, Jerusalem

258

257

259

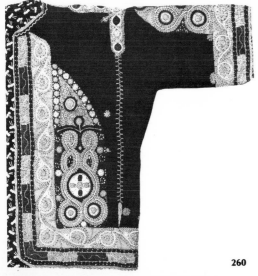

260

262

263

261

264

260 Woman's jacket (Taqsireh), Bethlehem
The material is blue velvet, with couching mainly in orange cord, with some green, purple, and gilt cord. Used for all festive occasions.

261 Detail of No. 260 (sleeve)

262 Detail of No. 260 (back panel)

263 Chest panel (Qabbeh), Bethlehem

264 Detail of sleeve panel of Bethlehem Taqsireh

265 Woman's jacket (Taqsireh), Bethlehem
The material is black velvet, with couching mainly in red, green, and yellow cord. Compared to plate No. 260, this piece of work falls short of its quality. Used for all festive occasions.

266   Chest panel (Qabbeh) from a dress (Thob Malek), Bethlehem
The dress fabric is coarse cotton. The chest panel is made of velvet and is sewn onto the dress after it is embroidered.

267   Detail of back panel of No. 265

268   Detail of sleeve of No. 265

269   Detail of sleeve of No. 266

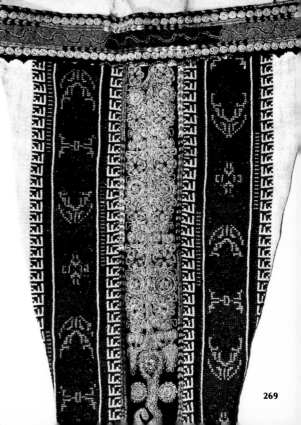

270

270 Old embroidery, Judean Hills, made into a jacket and lined with sheepskin

271 Adaptation of Bethlehem embroidery made into vests by Maskit

272 Adaptation of Bethlehem embroidery by Maskit
Done on coarse handwoven wool

273 Batik
Made by Laetitia Yalon

274 Batik
Made by Laetitia Yalon

275 Batik
Made by Laetitia Yalon

276 Batik
Made by Laetitia Yalon

277 Batik
Made by Laetitia Yalon

275

276

277

278

279

278 Batik
Made by Laetitia Yalon

279 Laetitia Yalon at work in her studio

280 Batik
Made by Laetitia Yalon

281 Batik
Made by Laetitia Yalon

282 Batik
Made by Laetitia Yalon

283 Batik
Made by Laetitia Yalon
Photo: Nat Suffrin

280

281

282

283

GIVE HER OF THE FRUIT OF HER

תנו־לה מפרי ידיה ויהללוה בשערים מעשיה:

OWN HANDS; AND LET HER WORKS

PRAISE HER IN THE GATES. PROVERBS 31:31

The aesthetic growth of any artist-craftsman is a matter of interest and importance, but to understand this development the details of the artist's life are essential. In this section a brief biography of one artist-craftsman is given. Meeting a craftsman makes it possible to know him as a student under the influence of instructors, or as a young artist on the threshold of a creative career, or as a mature, skilled, and experienced worker fully attuned to the creative forces of today. Meeting a craftsman also makes it possible to be aware of new blood and new influences that will undoubtedly contribute to Israel's culture.

The new artist-craftsmen who are recent immigrants are simply the latest wave of welcome arrivals. Within a short time Israel will enfold and assimilate their contributions into an even stronger burgeoning Israeli style and scene.

It is not enough for Israel to produce work merely indicative of the country itself; its crafts must be able to withstand comparison on an international level. Some of the Israeli work included in this book has met this challenge; other pieces are made by craftsmen striving for this world recognition.

Israelis absorb the influences of new and old, east and west, and town and country, mix them thoroughly, and distill their experiences into something exciting and completely reflective of the broad Israeli lifestyle. This art is neither narrow nor regional. The stimuli of inspiration are limitless: the entire land, spread out in all its wonder, allows the craftsman to make his contribution to the culture of the world.

One such international talent is Siona Shimshi, born in Tel Aviv in 1939 of Lithuanian parents. Siona studied at the Academy of Fine Arts in Tel Aviv and at Alfred University and Greenwich House Pottery in New York. She has worked as a painter, sculptress, and ceramist and as a textile designer has

7 WORKING

285   The craftsmanship of Siona Shimsi

created carpets, batik, and religious objects. She has shown her work in group and one-woman shows in New York, Tel Aviv, Jerusalem, and Paris. A truly creative individual and diversified designer, Siona has won many commissions for interior design on architectural projects in Israel.

When I asked Siona about herself and her work, she said: "I work in different media. Each medium answers a different sense of mine—the everyday and its traumatic experiences, the nights with strange dreams, perpetual motion. I am happy and excited when making my things but discontented when I look at my creation one year later. Perhaps I am trying to convert all the mud in the country into decorative walls, and the dull sheep's wool into rich, sensational carpets. I try desperately to help good taste to rule. I cannot solve people's problems; I can, at least, make them happy by making some beautiful things around them. In this way I hope to affect life here in Israel."

This then is Siona Shimshi, who is only one of many craftsmen who have built and are building a new tradition in style.

286

287

286 Working

287 "Orange Terminal"
El-Al Airlines, New York office
High-fired clay pillars (260 cm. high)

288A–B "All of Them My Boyfriends"
From a one-woman show called "Ten
Years Later"
High-fired clay (50 cm. high)

289 "All of Them My Boyfriends"
From a one-woman show called "Ten
Years Later"
High-fired clay (50 cm. high)

288A

288B

289

290

291

290 "Road Marker"
Gold leaf

291 "Trees"
High-fired clay (230 cm. high)

292 "Clay 'n' Cage"
30 cm. x 30 cm. x 30 cm.

293 "Clay Works"
High-fired clay (120 cm. high)

294

295

294 Ceramic wall

295 "All of Them My Boyfriends"
From a one-woman show called "Ten
Years Later"
High-fired clay (50 cm. high)

296 *Photo: A. Yaron*

296

297

298

297   Carpet wool

298   Detail of "Orange Terminal"

299   "Lots of Adams and Eves"
Batik (90 cm. x 250 cm.)
White, purple, black, and gold

300   "Clay Gater"
High-fired clay (250 cm. high)

301

301   "Wood Batik"
Four Seasons Hotel, Netanya, Israel

302   "Puppet Show" (closed)
High-fired clay (50 cm. high)

303   "Puppet Show" (opened, colorful inside)
High-fired clay (50 cm. high)

OVERLEAF
304 Original art work
Batik on paper, made with dyes
Designed by Siona Shimshi

302

303

305   **Works of Siona Shimshi**

306   **Works of Siona Shimshi**

A WORD FITLY SPOKEN IS LIKE

תפוחי זהב במשכיות כסף דבר דבר על־אפניו:

APPLES OF GOLD IN SETTINGS OF

SILVER. PROVERBS 25:11

307 Detail of "Rams" (No. 326)
Batik on cotton

8 MASKIT: ISRAEL'S CENTER OF HANDCRAFTS

In 1949 some friends asked me to visit a newly settled village in the Jerusalem area. It was a hot summer day, and during my visit I listened to complaints: no water for farming, burned fodder for the livestock, and many more. These were normal complaints for the newly arrived. Many hoped or expected that I could cure the age-old problems of building our homeland. As I returned to my home in Jerusalem, I was discouraged and truly upset. I thought, what could be done to lift the spirits of these women who were tied to parched patches of the earth? Most of the women were skilled in handcrafts, crafts that I had not seen displayed in the few shops that were in Israel at the time. As I thought, I became more and more excited about the idea of saving the crafts rather than solving the drought problem.

In 1954 Maskit was established as a government enterprise under the auspices of the Ministry of Labor. The name was chosen from the Bible; it means "ornament" or a "beautiful and aesthetically exciting object." The project was undertaken to encourage, safeguard, and provide a marketing outlet for the diverse folk crafts brought to Israel in the mass immigrations of people from seventy different countries. It was to encourage artisans to continue their native crafts in their new surroundings, to provide constructive livelihood in developed areas, to retain and safeguard the ancient crafts, and to present the crafts for sale to a discerning and discriminating public. From a beginning of only sixty workers in two villages, Maskit grew to employ over seven hundred people on a full- or part-time basis today. Some employees work in their own homes, some in central workshops; they work in the hills of Galilee, Nazareth, Jerusalem, Beersheba, and seventeen other cities and villages throughout the country.

There is a relatively new chapter in the story of Maskit, and this, too, is in

308

308 Wood characters and Noah's ark
Created by Frank Meisler
Photo: Zvi Steinberg

309 Batik on wood
Made by Natan Tal
Photo: Wilburt Feinberg

keeping with the basic spirit of the enterprise. As soon as it was practically possible after the Six Day War of 1967, the crafts of areas administered by Israel, where there were a large number of Arab workers, were incorporated into the framework of Maskit. Maskit even enlisted the help of production experts to advise in the development of Arab craftsmen so that they could take their place in the world market.

Many of the seven hundred weavers, silversmiths, and rug makers in Maskit are Israel's newcomers from the bazaars of Yemen and Persia; some come from the caves of Tripolitania, from towns in Tunisia, Kurdistan, and Morocco, as well as from dozens of European countries. The unique skill required for oriental hand weaving, rug making, embroidery, metalwork, ceramics, silver work, and jewelry has been revived by Maskit in modern Israel. Each craft is supervised by a professional expert on the Maskit staff, and this expert has helped merge ancient skills with the most modern western concepts of design, taste, and style. He also is responsible for supervising quality and introducing craftsmen to new methods and modern techniques.

As immigrating craftsmen have been absorbed and settled into the expanding Israeli economy, Maskit's initial goals have been met, maintained, and expanded. Hand-woven and embroidered classic and traditional garments, original accessories, hand-woven fabrics for upholstery, drapery, rugs of a variety of textures, jewelry, ceramics, glassware, and a large selection of gift items constitute the bulk of Maskit's production.

Dresses, robes, and other garments are fashioned of hand-woven fabrics of rich and varied hues indigenous to Israel and are particularly designed for winter wear. Lighter-weight summer fabrics are also made into exclusive designs created for Maskit by leading artists, textile designers, and tailor-seamstresses. The

310

311

312
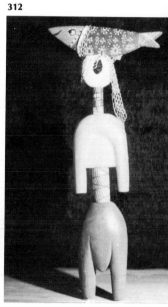

313

310–319   "Dolls"
Made by Ruth Sternshuss

314

315

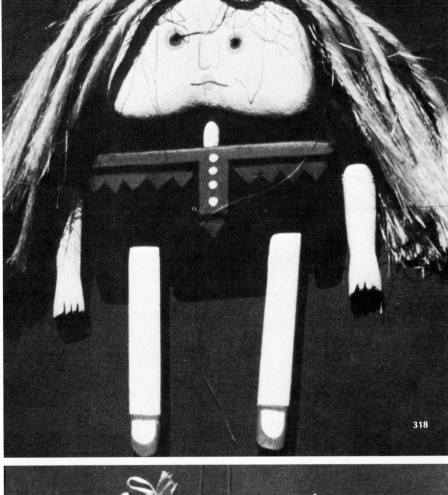

318

316

317

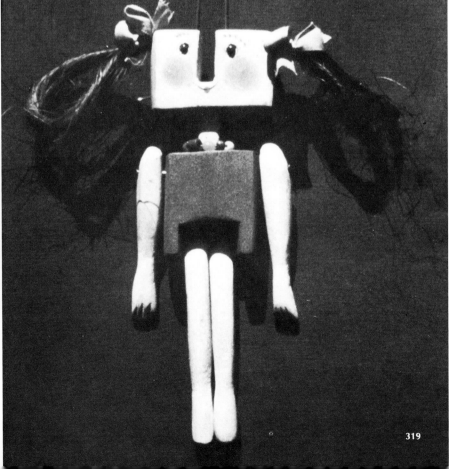

319

fabrics in all the fashions are made of home-grown Israeli wool and cotton.

Modern local artists have been encouraged to participate in and contribute to Maskit's endeavors to develop an Israeli style in the arts and crafts. Thus, Maskit exists to initiate, produce, buy, and sell Israeli handcrafts. The value of each item is determined by the materials used, as well as the imagination, experience, and skill of execution, which are the main ingredients in the creation of each finished product. Export of Maskit products to major specialty shops all over the world has met with resounding success.

Other Maskit activities include the initiation and sponsoring of exhibits and the commissioning of work by designers and artists. A new gallery, Maskit Shesh, located in the El Al Building in Tel Aviv, has been opened for promoting and expanding the field of decorative arts. The main showrooms of Maskit are in Tel Aviv, with branches in Jerusalem and other cities and towns throughout Israel. There is also a showroom and wholesale showroom at 55 West Fifty-fifth Street in New York City.

320 Toy boat
Made by Ruth Sternshuss

321 "Bedouin Mother and Children"
Made by Ruth Sternshuss

322–323 "Dolls"
Made by Ruth Sternshuss

320

321

322

323

324   "Pregnant Woman"
Batik on cotton
Made by Alexandra Zaid
Photo: Yaki Molho

325   "The Lady in Blue"
Batik on cotton
Made by Alexandra Zaid
Photo: Yaki Molho

326   "Rams"
Batik on cotton (60 cm. x 90 cm.)
Made by Nitza Shimshoni

327   "Woman in Orange"
Batik on cotton (60 cm. x 90 cm.)
Made by Nitza Shimshoni
Photo: Yaki Molho

324   325

326

327

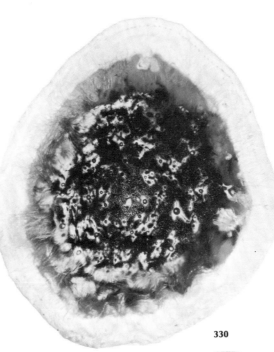

329

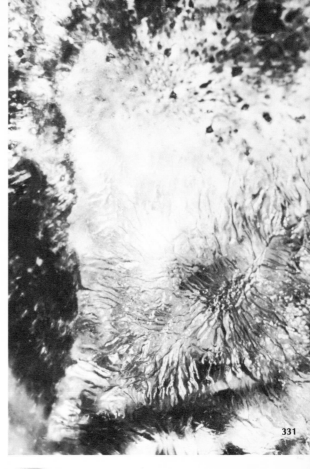

331

330

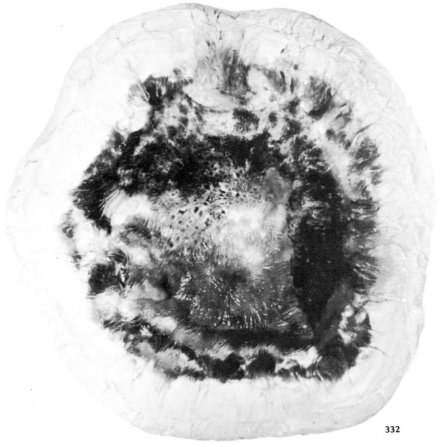

328 "Gobelin Tapestry"
Designed by Yochanan Simon
Executed by George Goldstein
Workshop, Jerusalem
Photo: Israel Zafrir

329 Detail of No. 330
Made by Chila Bar-Tal
Photo: Yaki Molho

330 Glass bowl (yellow)
Laminated glass
Made by Chila Bar-Tal
Photo: Yaki Molho

331 Detail of No. 332
Made by Chila Bar-Tal
Photo: Yaki Molho

332 Glass bowl (blue)
Made by Chila Bar-Tal
Photo: Yaki Molho

332

---

333   Glass vase
Handblown and designed by Ariel
Bar-Tal
Photo: Wilburt Feinberg

334   Glass vase
Handblown and designed by Ariel
Bar-Tal
Photo: Wilburt Feinberg

335   Glass vases
Handblown and designed by Ariel
Bar-Tal
Photo: Wilburt Feinberg

336   Glass vase
Handblown and designed by Ariel
Bar-Tal
Photo: Wilburt Feinberg

336

335

SO THE CHILDREN OF ISRAEL DID

‫. . . כן עשו בני ישראל את כל־העבודה:‬

ALL THE WORK. EXODUS 39:42

337 Yemenite woman making baskets
(c. 1952)

To say that newcomers at the time of the greatest immigration to the new state of Israel more than twenty years ago brought with them many and diverse talents has become something of an abstraction and a generalization. But my involvement with this field was no abstraction at all; much of it started with two very specific and rather dirty little pieces of cloth that came to me in quite different ways and both of which had been woven in distant exotic places.

At the time it all began I was working as a volunteer occupational expert in the immigrant villages in the Jerusalem area. These villages were hurriedly assembled under conditions that would today seem extremely primitive. They had been built as quickly as possible to house the waves of newcomers from Europe and Asia. My work was to provide instruction in agriculture. I was, as it happens, a trained and experienced farmer, and the national policy at that time was to settle these immigrants, many of whom had never seen, much less lived on, a farm in their entire lives, and help them become farmers.

As it happened, my assignment did not work out as planned. We soon discovered that economically viable agricultural activity was not feasible at that moment (although later it did work out, and unfortunately at the expense of arts and crafts). In my travels to the struggling settlements I discovered, to my delight, samples of handcrafts that these immigrants had made and brought from their previous homes. These were not "designed" artifacts (those came later, with more sophisticated immigrants) but rather things such as jewelry, rugs, and garments made by hand and used in the home or worn. These handcrafts were part of everyday life. I was overjoyed by this discovery; these objects were, in fact, the start of Maskit.

All my life I have loved making

things with my hands, and since childhood I have found great pleasure in knitting, crocheting, embroidery, and craft work, but I never expected that my life would eventually come to be professionally absorbed in handcrafts. And it was all the result of the failure of an agricultural settlement, a failure in agriculture, which was what I really had been trained for as a young girl.

Let us return to those two pieces of dirty cloth because they tell an interesting part of the story. One was finely woven—almost like gossamer—in an intricate pattern of white, black, and red. The other, much more rugged and more typical of the weaving techniques of newcomers from primitive areas, was boldly striped in many hues. The delicate gossamer type of cloth had been woven far underground by a unique tribe of Jews in a place called Garian, in Libya, where the entire community lived in huge caves below the surface of the desert. These Jews had recently come to Israel and were settled in a village called Porat, near Natanya. The more coarsely woven piece of cloth had been made in southern Arabia by a small community of Jews who had lived in friendly relations with the surrounding Arab majority; the place of their origin was an obscure area called Bayhan, near Yemen, and their new home was a tent city near Jerusalem.

Both of these discoveries developed in unexpected ways. Our immediate problem with the gossamerlike cloth from the Garian cave dwellers, which was used for prayer shawls, was to find a way in which it could be sold for a price that would compensate the hours of labor that went into its fabrication, when no reasonable selling price could possibly cover the investment of time. After all, the point of our whole evolving craft project was to develop products and markets that could help newcomers to supplement their living in their new homes, although Israel in those days was far from affluent. In Libya these Jews had

9 OUR PEOPLE

338   Porat rug making (c. 1950)
Photo: Werner Braun

not really lived in a money economy as we know it; there the women of the community did not help with the primitive farming of the men, as is usually the custom. Instead, the women devoted most of their time to weaving (usually done by the men in the sub-Sahara regions) and in this way were able to develop their craft to a higher form than is usually seen.

We solved the problem by "exaggeration." That is, we planned new ways of executing the traditional work so that it could be produced on a larger scale and with coarser fibers. With the same time and effort, the weaver produced far more yardage. Instead of prayer shawls, the weavers came up with rugs. This principle of "exaggeration" was one that had been used only a short time earlier with a group of newcomers from Bulgaria. The Bulgarian women did beautiful traditional embroidery, which was used on curtains and bedspreads. It was suggested that they enlarge the scale of their work to achieve an effect that was bold rather than delicate. They used the same patterns, and the results were exquisite handbags.

With the use of this technique the unique distinction of the Garian weaving, of course, was preserved. It was a matter of fiber and dye: natural white cotton, natural white mohair, and natural black taken from black goats were spun into threads and then woven into patterns. The dye used was made from pomegranates, one of the native fruits of Israel. When the completed fabric was dipped in the dye bath, the white mohair threads absorbed the pomegranate dye and turned a bright rust red, while the natural white cotton threads did not absorb this particular dye and remained white and, of course, the black remained black. The finished work was thus always in these three traditional colors.

The entire question of using synthetic fibers and dyes later came to pose a serious dilemma. We are still trying to retain the use of natural fibers in our Maskit production, but it is difficult to continue against the encroachment of synthetic fibers. On the question of dyes we had to give in. While by inclination I would far prefer to stay with the old, traditional, natural vegetable dyes, I am forced to admit that most natural or plant-organic dyes are not color fast. The natural dyes must often be set chemically, and the immigrants who, in the countries of their origin, were familiar with and used these chemicals, which were probably found in the minerals in nature (as in Gaza, where the dyed fibers are washed and set in sea water, which helps to set the color, although sea water does not make the dye satisfactorily color fast), simply could not, even with our help, find comparable materials in Israel. So now, reluctantly, we have our rugs and other fabrics dyed in factories with synthetic chemical or aniline dyes. However, we are usually guided by the color vibrancy and hue of a natural dye.

Incidentally, today the weavers from the Libyan caves have given up the handcraft of their primitive past and are now a prosperous agricultural community. In their case, the phase of hand looming in Israel might be described as a transitional stopgap until their new life of modernized and mechanized farming became a reality.

By contrast, the weavers of the boldly striped piece of cloth, whose discovery led me to the Jews of Bayhan in southern Arabia, have continued their handcraft work until this very day, and not only are they weaving but they are also working in jewelry, another of their traditional crafts. These immigrants, who had enjoyed a uniquely comfortable life as respected craftsmen among the Arabs, were living in conditions of extreme squalor in a tent city near Jerusalem when we first met over twenty years ago. I was shocked and depressed by the situation, but it was soon improved when Prime Minister Ben-Gurion ordered the Israeli army to move into the area and to function not as a military task force but as a public health resource. It was to bring order, hygiene, and progress to this community. Even within the disorder and dirt of the tent city I could not help noticing the brightly striped robes the people were wearing, and I asked whether they might weave more of this fabric for our project. They agreed with modest delight and did the job in much less time that I had requested. And so a new-old work in handcraft began.

Among the newcomers who did that first weaving assignment were two young men who have been working at Maskit for most of the years since then—Haim Ben-David and his cousin Moshe Ben-David. Moshe is an expert weaver and Haim a skilled and devoted jeweler. During the years they have told me stories of their lives in Arabia, where, as Moshe put it, the sharif, or local ruler, respected and admired the Jews of his community because they were not merchants merely interested in money but artists deeply involved in their crafts of jewelry-making and weaving.

Haim, in fact, had been the sharif's private jeweler, assigned to make special gifts—an ornate sheath for a dagger or sword, for instance—when the ruler wanted to impress an important friend or a British officer. Although he lost an eye at the age of five, when he was helping his jeweler father do filigree work and was blinded by a thread of silver metal, his artistry is unimpaired. His roots in the inherited traditions of the craft have not been lost. Today he can work in many styles, but always interpreting his craft through the origins that are part of him into work whose feeling may be European and romantic or functionally modern in style.

At the same time that Haim and Moshe and their kinsmen were arriving in Israel, other immigrants from equally far-flung points were arriving as well, each bringing talents to a country that at

339   Moshe Ben-David (c. 1950)

340   Moshe Ben-David (today)
Photo: Jaacov Agor

339

340

341 Porat carding wool (c. 1950)
Photo: Werner Braun

342 Rug woven at Porat (c. 1950)

341

the time had very little in the way of native artistry. It must be remembered that the values of Israel in those years were all directed toward the essential needs of farming, building, and modernization. Rapid growth and dynamic changes were part of the changing standard of living.

The Arab countries, Israel's neighbors, possess far richer resources in handwork than we do. A hundred years ago, before any serious immigration of Jews to Palestine, the exquisite embroidery of Arab women in the remote and small villages was taken for granted; with the technological development brought by the Jews came a related decline in handcrafts. This process of decline in craftwork is taking place throughout the world as industrialization brings higher wages and makes many of the traditional craftwork items obsolete.

The mass immigration, particularly from North Africa and Asia, brought special skills we simply had not known. The immigrants of the early 1950s were bringing their skills into something of an artistic vacuum. We simply had not been thinking in terms of arts or crafts, for we had been too busy building and defending the country. It was only somewhat later that the immigration of sophisticated artists and designers from Europe who worked in terms of "designed" crafts came to further enrich our lives.

Among the jewelers, for instance, were silversmiths from Hadhramaut, also a section of southern Arabia, who hammered their special style of work out of the Maria Theresa thaler, an old European coin made of an alloy of silver that is softer and more workable than pure silver and which, being very decorative, was in use as the currency of the region. These people, steeped in superstition, used such silver items as boxes to hold charms. We at Maskit changed the design a bit, and one of these boxes, whose forerunner I had

watched being hammered out in a hovel over twenty years ago, is a design still being made for sale at Maskit.

Other examples of the Hadhramaut jewelry were the massive belts and necklaces worn by the women. Some of these elaborate pieces weigh as much as forty-five pounds and were part of a traditional wedding outfit. Again we used the "exaggeration" principle, and after long and difficult discussion with the craftsmen, who could not understand why we wanted to interfere with their age-old ways of doing things, they began to produce jewelry pieces suitable for modern women in western-style dress, using only one or two of the elements of the massive arrangements that were originally assembled.

From Algeria came an entire family of silversmiths who specialized in a type of filigree that is unusually graceful, airy, and intricate. The family, all of whom are deaf-mutes, continue their work to this day. Maskit has adapted their imaginative designs for use in contemporary items, such as cigarette cases or pillboxes.

From Jerba, an island off the coast of North Africa forming part of Tunisia, known to the Greeks and Romans as the "Island of the Lotus-Eaters," came a community of Jews skilled in the technique of enameling metal, something practically unknown in Israel. This family used enamel to make beads for women's jewelry—all sorts of beads, round, square, oval-shaped—all executed with an unusual cloisonné finish. This technique, too, we found could be adapted beautifully to make decorative containers.

These same Jews of Jerba also made rugs, as well as other types of jewelry. In fact, rug and jewelry-making were the basic mainstays of crafts in this area since, with pottery, they provided most of the furnishings and objects of everyday life. No line was drawn between the beautiful, the decorative, and the necessary. The rugs of Jerba had

342

one unusual feature: they were never rectangular, with parallel sides, but rather became narrower from one end to the other. The wide end was where the weaver began his work, and the narrow end was the last section. For all the years of tradition and usage these craftsmen, like similar ones in Persia, never developed the barlike reed that holds the warp threads parallel and keeps the warp from drawing closer together as the pressure of the weft increases. We provided this simple device, and now the rugs of Jewish craftsmen from Jerba have parallel edges.

Rugs made by Jews from Morocco are distinctive in color and design. They are quite modern-looking but actually are deeply traditional, often using the black and white pattern of the Berbers. The rugs made by Jews from Azerbaijan were related to the famous carpets of Persia, of which they were simple rustic versions. I met these newcomers, living in a cluttered village in their new home in Galilee, where they were weaving rugs for their own use; the hand-knotted carpets were made on their horizontal looms using vegetable-dyed threads. The skills were traditional, but the patterns were not distinguished or suitable for sale.

Here again the problem was how to combine the traditional methods of fabrication with a design that would meet contemporary needs. We had no designers at Maskit at that time, but an interior decorator suggested that we try plain, solid-color, unadorned rugs. Interestingly enough, this idea did not appeal to the villagers and they refused to do it. They said such weaving was too boring. Only one woman agreed to use the wools I brought to the village, and she made one plain rug—but she was unable to resist adding a border of flowers around the edge.

During one of my early visits to the Galilee village of these Azerbaijan Jews, I brought along the vice-president of B. Altman, the New York City department

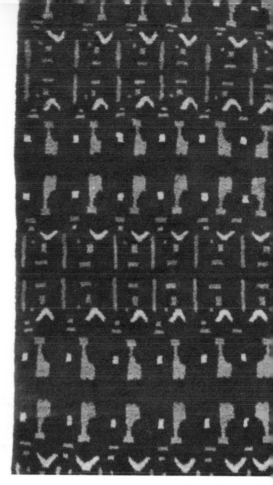

343 A–E   Rugs woven at Porat (c. 1950)

343A

34

store, who had been on a buying trip in Persia. He had been looking at Persia's beautiful rugs, of which our villagers' work was merely a rough approximation. He suggested that we use the services of experts to design modern patterns for the rugs—vivid stripes on plain backgrounds. This we did, and the artist Jean David, then a new immigrant from Romania, worked out fifty different variations in a variety of well-balanced color schemes. This turned out to be an excellent solution—a good example of the interplay between a sophisticated designer who understood the taste of the western world and the skilled craftsmen whose fingers could work carpeting knots. Both designer and craftsmen were new immigrants at the time. They combined their talents and created a product new and satisfactory to both.

Even my daughter Yael became a

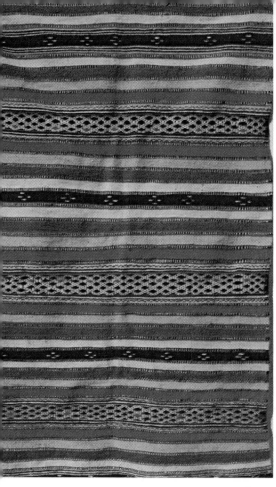

343C   343D   343E

designer for Maskit. At the age of fourteen, she accompanied the archaeologist Nelson Glueck on a dig in the Negev and the party discovered ancient rock drawings, including one of an ibex. Yael drew a design of the discovery and added Hebrew lettering. It became the pattern of a rug made by the villagers and is one of the designs still in production today.

A far more sophisticated weaving technique was brought to us by a new immigrant from Iraq whose prosperous Baghdad factory had fifty looms producing Harris tweed fabric for export to England. Soon after he arrived, penniless, in Israel, word of his background and experience came to my office at the Labor Ministry. We went about building looms and setting more new immigrants to work—not, to be sure, turning out Harris tweeds but instead manufacturing distinctive and unusual designs using new combinations of materials with wool. One design, for example, uses leather strips. This project is still in operation, turning out custom-designed hand-woven fabrics for Maskit fashions.

This has been only an overview of what have been the crafts of Israel. Who would have dreamed that such a diversified people would find one another during our lifetime and accelerate the slow process of time to help provide better lives for the artists and craftsmen as well as for the buyers of handcrafts. And who would have believed it possible to capture primitive techniques, styles, motifs, colors, and excitement into modern, usable, wearable objects of decoration, of garments of flair and fashion for an entire new world and life style.

10 A CROSS SECTION OF ISRAELI CRAFTS AND CRAFTSMEN

Ariel Bar-Tal

Born in 1920 in Budapest, where he learned drawing and painting as a schoolboy. Prevented by the prewar regime in Hungary from completing his studies at the Academy of Fine Arts, he turned to glassblowing of scientific apparatus as a practical occupation. After spending the war years in concentration camps, he went to Rome. There he completed his artistic training, studying sculpture and the history of arts and crafts and at the same time working as a scientific glassblower.

He settled in Israel in 1950 and has the distinction of being "the first artistic glassblower" since Roman times to again awake from the long sleep "a glass vessel of such artistic beauty and sculptural quality." He has had exhibitions at Tiffany's, New York; the Haaretz Museum, Tel Aviv; and other one-man shows

Hanna Charag-Zuntz

Born in 1915 in Germany. From 1935 to 1940 she studied pottery with Siegfried Müller and afterward in other centers of Germany, as well as in Prague, Teplitzschöne, and Florence. She immigrated to Israel in 1940 and worked with Hedwig Grossman in Jerusalem until 1942. She produces independently in her own studio on Mount Carmel in Haifa. Aside from her studio work she is also engaged in teaching her craft and in designing industrial pottery at the Art Institute of Teachers Seminary (Oranim) and at courses for Industrial Design at the Israel Institute of Technology (Technion), Haifa. She has had many exhibitions and her works have been purchased by a number of museums and private collections in the United States, England, Italy, Germany, Japan, and Israel. She has also won many prizes for her work.

Kopel Gurwin

Born in Vilna in 1923, was educated there at a center of Hebrew culture. His studies were interrupted by World War II, which he spent in concentration camps. On being liberated, he went to Sweden, where he stayed for five years before immigrating to Israel in 1950. He completed his studies at the Bezalel School in Jerusalem in 1957 and has been actively associated with the field of graphic and artistic creation in Israel ever since. Appliqué banners, which he started producing in 1966, have now become his main form of artistic expression.

The work of Kopel Gurwin frequently has a pastoral quality, with high decorative impact. In other examples of his work he injects a simple narrative with humor and strong symbolism. He has been awarded many prizes.

Leon Israel

Born in 1943 and immigrated to Israel in 1955. After completing his army service, he continued his education at the Bezalel School in Jerusalem, where he majored in jewelry and metal arts. He graduated with honors in 1969. After finishing his studies at Bezalel, he traveled and designed jewelry for firms in Europe and the United States. In December 1970 he was awarded honorable mention in the annual Jewel of the Year competition held by the Israel Export Institute. In 1971 Leon Israel became the first Israeli to be awarded the Diamond International Award by the world-known De Beers diamond corporation.

Amitai Kav

A sabra (native), born in 1941 and grew up in Kibbutz Negba in the Negev Desert. In 1946 he left the kibbutz and studied dance in Jerusalem. For three years he wrote notations for movement in dance using the system of Noa Eshkol. He has studied fine art for two years in Tel Aviv and learned his craft as a model maker and through experimentation. He has had no formal schooling for jewelry making. Amitai Kav never uses the casting technique for his jewelry but prefers to draw the design, which he considers "finished," on paper. He then cuts and files the pieces separately. Each finished piece is unique, and rather than repeat a piece, Amitai prefers making variations. He usually has "families" of jewelry consisting of about four to five pieces. Influences of his dance and fine arts background are discernible in his approach to jewelry design.

Hana Kralova

Arrived in Israel in March 1965 from Czechoslovakia. She immediately started to work and met with overwhelming success and appreciation for her fine work. In Czechoslovakia, Hana studied interior textile design in Prague at the University for Applied Art. She worked as the chief designer for bobbin lace work at the Center for People's Art, Prague. In Israel she has revived the centuries-old art, and she has world exhibitions to her credit: Montreal (at Expo '67), Brussels, Chile, Canada, Florence, Budapest, Moscow. There has been so much interest generated by Hana Kralova that she has started a course for the teaching of bobbin lace art.

Shulamit Litan

Born in 1936 in Poland and arrived in Israel the same year. She has had no formal schooling but has been working most of her life in various art media. After years of "free painting" she began to work with textiles and creating designs from scraps of leather. Her first attempt was to perfect batik. After her success she then went on to appliqué and stitchery, which were done mainly for ceremonial objects, then for fashion and decoration. She now combines several techniques in her work, which are batik, quilting, stitchery, and printing.

Shulamit says about her work: "I love the rich oriental coloring, the ornamental and flowing line and I believe in good craftsmanship." She has had exhibitions in Europe, the United States, and Israel, and in 1966 and 1969 her work was shown in Stuttgart's Internationales Kunsthandwork.

Daniel Nahum

Born in Milan, Italy, in 1925. In his youth he showed a talent for art and studied at the Accademia Albertina in Turin under the guidance of the painter Felite Casorati. During World War II he took an active part in the resistance fighting and served with the partisans of the Fourth Brigade Garibaldi. In 1950 he immigrated to Israel and settled as a member of Kibbutz Ruhama, on the border of the Negev Desert, where he still lives.

Daniel has had many exhibitions and commissions for his work, and in 1968 he was awarded second prize at the Twenty-sixth International Competition of Ceramics in Faenza, Italy. In 1968–69 he created a monumental bas-relief (fifty square meters of surface) decorating the hall of the Hotel Ivoire in Abidjan, Ivory Coast. From 1969–71 he taught at the Ecole des Arts in Abidjan.

Arieh Ophir

A sabra born in Kibbutz Beit-Nir at the top of the Negev Desert. He came to silver while undergoing rehabilitation for a wound he received while serving in the army. Upon being released from the hospital, he went to perfect his craft and studied at Bezalel School in Jerusalem. Upon graduation he received a grant to study in Copenhagen with Georg Jensen, and on his return to Israel opened his workshop in the Jerusalem House of Quality. He now heads the silversmith and metal arts department at the Bezalel Academy of Arts and Design, Jerusalem.

Although Arieh's style is modern, as his work shows, he maintains and respects tradition and custom in religious objects. He is actively involved in the organization and development of the craftsman's place in Israel and the world's society.

Kurt Pfeffermann

Born in Germany in 1919 and came to Israel in 1939. A most exacting craftsman with a very definite approach to design and execution of his work, he has maintained the traditional European design concepts and has introduced the feelings that one acquires when living in Israel. The list of his awards and prizes is very long, and among his most coveted is the 1962 gold medal, Bavarian State Award for Jewelry at the International Exhibition of Arts and Crafts, special section, "Form + Quality," in Munich. He has participated in international exhibitions in Jerusalem, Munich, Stuttgart, Toronto, New York, San Francisco, Florence, Stockholm, Goeteborg, Los Angeles, Bern, Frankfurt, Berlin, Haifa, and Tel Aviv.

Lidia Zavadsky

Born in 1937 in Poland, where she took her master's in law. She came to Israel in 1961 and studied ceramics at the Bezalel Academy of Art and Design in Jerusalem, where she was awarded the graduation prize. In 1965 she opened her studio in Jerusalem and since then has exhibited her work throughout Israel. In 1971–72 she had a one-woman show at the Ceramics Museum, Museum Haaretz, Tel Aviv.

Exhibitions abroad in which she participated include Expo '67 in Montreal and the International Competition of Artistic Ceramics in Faenza, Italy. In 1969 she was awarded first prize and shared second prize at the Competition for Designing Ceramic Lamps sponsored by the Ministry of Commerce and Industry. In 1971 she was elected titular member of the International Academy of Ceramics, UNESCO. Lidia at present teaches ceramics at Bezalel.